THE SCANDAL OF CHRISTINE KEELER AND JOHN PROFUMO

'The repackaging of classics is a tried and trusted winner, but Tim Coates has come up with something entirely original: the repackaging of history. He has transformed papers [from archives] … into verbatim narratives, so, for instance, in UFOs in the House of Lords we get a hilarious recreation, directly from Hansard, of a nutty debate that took place in 1979 … This is inspired publishing, not only archivally valuable but capable of bringing the past back to life without the usual filter of academic or biographer.' Guardian

'It is difficult to praise the idea, the format, the selection and the quality of the series too highly.' Times Higher Education Supplement

'Who, outside a few historians, knows that the British invaded Tibet? We approach these stories with an immediacy it would be impossible to contrive … from one of the richest unexplored attics in the country.' Robert Winder, The Independent

THE SCANDAL OF CHRISTINE KEELER AND JOHN PROFUMO

Lord Denning's Report, 1963

MOMENTS OF HISTORY

Series editor: Tim Coates

TIM COATES

London and New York

Applications for reproduction should be made in writing to Tim Coates, c/o Littlehampton Book Services, Durrington, West Sussex BN13 3RB, UK or c/o Midpoint Trade Books, 27 West 20th Street, Suite 1102, New York, NY 10011, USA.

ISBN 1 84381 024 7

The material for this book is drawn from The Controller's Library of The Stationery Office in London. TSO have generously given access to the Library for the content of this series.
First published by HMSO in 1963 as Cmnd. 2152
© Crown copyright.
This selection and this edition © Tim Coates.

A CIP catalogue record for this book is available from the British Library.

Editor: Frances Maher
Photographs: Cecilia Weston-Baker
Cover design: David Carroll and Sarah Theodosiou
Design: Sarah Theodosiou
Manufactured in Singapore by Imago
Series Editor: Tim Coates

Cover photograph © Bettmann/CORBIS: Christine Keeler, July 1963
Inside front cover © Hulton|Archive: John Profumo and his wife, the former actress Valerie Hobson, 1962
Inside back cover © Charles O'Rear/CORBIS: Big Ben and the Thames River, London

About the series

Moments of History are historic official papers which have not previously been available in a popular form. They have been chosen for the quality of their story-telling and are illustrated with contemporary photographs and drawings. Some subjects are familiar, but others are less well known. Each is a moment in history. A complete list of this and the associate series *uncovered editions* is to be found at the back of this book. Further details are available on www.timcoatesbooks.com.

About the series editor, Tim Coates

Tim Coates studied at University College, Oxford and at the University of Stirling. After working in the theatre for a number of years, he took up bookselling and became managing director, firstly of Sherratt and Hughes bookshops, and then of Waterstone's. He is known for his support for foreign literature, particularly from the Czech Republic, and specializes in the republishing of interesting archives. The idea for *uncovered editions* came while searching through the bookshelves of his late father-in-law, Air Commodore Patrick Cave OBE. Tim Coates is married to Bridget Cave, has two sons and lives in London. He is the author of *The Lady in the Case: The Romances of Patsy Cornwallis West* to be published by Bloomsbury in 2003.

Tim Coates welcomes views and ideas on the *Moments of History* and *uncovered editions* series.

He can be e-mailed at timcoatesbooks@yahoo.com.

The publishers would like to thank the photographers and organizations for their kind permission to reproduce the photographs in this book.

Every effort has been made to trace the holders of any copyright material included in this book. However, if there are any omissions we will be happy to rectify them in future editions.

Copyright in illustrations is as follows:

CORBIS, London:
Bettman – pp. iv, xii (bottom left), 88, 160
Macduff Everton – p. 10
Michael Freeman – p. 186 (bottom left)
Hulton-Deutsch Collection – pp. xii (top right), 5, 58, 162
Douglas Kirkland – p. 186 (top right)
Geray Sweeney – p. 186 (top left)

Hulton | Archive, London – pp. ix, x, xii (bottom right and top left), xv, 2, 7, 17, 19, 23, 30, 36, 42, 69, 74, 81, 93, 99, 104, 115, 124, 126, 137, 147, 154, 169, 177

Magnum Photos, London:
Eve Arnold – p. 186 (bottom right)

John Frost Historical Newspapers, London – pp. xvi, 122

Mandy Rice-Davies (centre, right) and Christine Keeler (behind) surrounded by press photographers as they leave the Old Bailey during the trial of Stephen Ward, 22 July 1963

1963 was in many ways a pivotal year in a pivotal decade – not only in the United Kingdom but also in the United States of America and throughout the world, in government and in society, in entertainment and in travel.

When British Prime Minister Harold Macmillan used the phrase 'the wind of change is blowing' in February 1960, he was referring to the growth of national consciousness in the continent of Africa. And shortly afterwards the massacre of 56 innocent people in a demonstration at Sharpeville in the Transvaal led to the UN Security Council calling on the South African government 'to abandon its policies of apartheid and racial discrimination' (Resolution 134, April 1960). However, Macmillan's words were prophetic of a much deeper change in the establishment of power, particularly in his own country.

The first three years of the 'Swinging Sixties' saw the rise of a boxing legend – Cassius Clay; the election of the youngest president of the USA – John F. Kennedy; the birth of a new soap opera – Coronation Street; an Old Bailey jury's approval of a D.H. Lawrence novel – Lady Chatterley's Lover; a major breakthrough for 20th century women – the contraceptive pill; the unveiling of a new Jaguar – the E-type; the first person in space – Major Yuri Gagarin; the Soviet bloc turning up the heat in the Cold War – the building of the Berlin Wall, virtually overnight; the sentencing to death of one of Hitler's most important henchmen – Adolf Eichmann; the musical faux pas of the century – Decca turning down the Beatles; the first American to orbit the earth – John Glenn; the birth of a satirical magazine – Private Eye; the first Sunday newspaper colour supplement in Britain – The Sunday Times; the means of the first TV pictures across the Atlantic – Telstar; the death of a Hollywood icon – Marilyn Monroe; America and Russia on the brink of a nuclear war – the Cuban Missile Crisis; the jailing for five years of a future South African president – Nelson Mandela (who would stand trial for treason in 1964); an agreement between France and the UK to build a supersonic airliner – Concord.

ACHTUNG
100 m
Schweizer Grenze

607

HALT

WH-133

What would 1963 bring?

Beeching and the Beatles: Despite almost unanimous opposition, the report of British Railways Chairman Dr Beeching led to the closure of more than 2,000 stations and put almost 68,000 people out of a job. Beatlemania arrived – screaming fans of George Harrison, John Lennon, Paul McCartney and Ringo Starr caused havoc at airports and elsewhere and 'She Loves You' was at number one in the charts for four weeks.

Martin Luther King and John F. Kennedy: Campaigning for racial equality, Martin Luther King (assassinated in 1968) made his famous 'I have a dream' speech. President John F. Kennedy, aged 46 – and just five months after his moving address to the people of Berlin in which he said 'Ich bin ein Berliner' – was assassinated in November in Dallas, Texas, to the horror of the world.

Charles de Gaulle and Winston Churchill: de Gaulle vetoed Britain's entry into the European Economic Community. Churchill, aged 88 and 60 years an MP, announced he would not stand at the next election.

The Organization of African Unity and the Nuclear Test-Ban Treaty: The OAU was founded by representatives of 30 African governments meeting in Addis Ababa, Ethiopia. In Moscow Britons, Americans and Russians toasted 'peace and friendship among nations' at the signing of the treaty banning nuclear weapon tests in the atmosphere, outer space and underwater.

Harold Macmillan and Harold Wilson: Macmillan resigned as prime minister and was succeeded by Lord Douglas Home. Harold Wilson was elected leader of the Labour Party.

The Great Train Robbery – 'the crime of the century': In the early hours of 8th August 1963 a gang of at least 15 men stopped and attacked the Glasgow to London mail train near Leighton Buzzard in Buckinghamshire and made off with 120 mailbags containing almost £2.6 million, a staggering amount of money at that time.

From Russia with Love and The Great Escape: The second, hugely successful, James Bond film came out in May. The feature film of the

In the news in 1963 (clockwise from top right): police in Buckingham-shire, The Beatles, *The Great Escape* with Steve McQueen, John F. Kennedy and family. Related *Moments of History* titles are *The Great British Train Robbery, John Lennon: the FBI files, Escaping from Germany, The Shooting of John F. Kennedy.*

great escape – from the prisoner-of-war camp Stalag Luft III in 1944 – was based on the book of one of the survivors, starred Steve McQueen and still retains its popularity.

William Vassall and Kim Philby: A tribunal chaired by Lord Radcliffe was set up to investigate the circumstances that led to the jailing for 18 years of the Admiralty clerk John Vassall, a homosexual who had been blackmailed into spying for the KGB. Philby was revealed as the 'third man' in the Burgess and Maclean spy scandal.

The biggest scandal ever to hit British politics was, however, the Profumo affair. On 4 June 1963 John Profumo, the Secretary of State for War and a Conservative MP since 1940, resigned after he was found to be having an affair with a call-girl who had associations with a Russian naval officer. Harold Macmillan, the British Prime Minister, invited Lord Alfred Denning, a senior judge, to undertake an inquiry into the circumstances leading to the resignation, to investigate any information or material which came to his attention in this connection and to consider any evidence for believing that national security had been or might have been endangered.

Lord Denning's report, reproduced here, was eagerly awaited by the public and over 100,000 copies were sold in the first three days after publication. Described as the raciest and most readable Blue Book (Parliamentary report) ever published, it portrays the extraordinary sexual behaviour of the ruling classes in the 1960s and addresses many of the rumours that were rife and affected 'the honour and integrity of public life'. The report is also noteworthy in that, for the first time, it revealed publicly the role and responsibilities of the Security Service.

Lord Denning in Horse Guards' Parade, 16 September 1963, the day his report was delivered to the prime minister

Sunday Mirror
AND SUNDAY PICTORIAL

5d. June 9, 1963 No. 10 * * *

PROFUMO
HIS LETTER TO
CHRISTIN

9/8/

Darling

In great haste & because I can get no reply from your phone—

Alas something's blown up tomorrow night and I can't therefore make it. I'm terribly sorry especially as I leave the next day for various trips & then a holiday so won't be able to see you again until some time in September. Blast it. Please take great care of yourself & don't run away

Love J.

I'm writing this 'cos I know you're off the day tomorrow & I want you to know before you go if I still can't reach you by phone

F OR some months a rumour has been buzzing around Those In The Know about a letter written by the Right Honourable John Dennis Profumo, Privy Councillor.

[A Privy Councillor is one of the Queen's "right trusty and well beloved" advisers.]

Mr. Profumo was the Tory Secretary of State for War until the British public studied their newspapers on Thursday morning.

According to the rumour Mr. Profumo's letter was addressed to Miss Christine Keeler, who no longer needs to be introduced or described to anybody who isn't blind or deaf.

Rumour Correct

It has also been said that The Letter was, or had been, in the possession of a national newspaper.

Today the Sunday Mirror can emphatically state:

1 The rumour is correct.

2 The letter was written by Mr. John Profumo.

3 It was addressed to Miss Christine Keeler and began with the word "Darling." It was signed: "Love, J."

Now that the War Minister has resigned after confessing an association with Christine Keeler, it is possible to explain why this letter was not published, and precisely what happened to it.

In January, after a shooting incident at the West End flat of Dr. Stephen Ward, Miss Keeler, a 20-year-old model from Staines, was in touch with the Sunday Pictorial concerning

her story of how she had been involve[d] society life of London.

During the talks with a Pictorial rep[re] alleged that among the men with w[hom] had had affairs were Mr. John Profum[o] Russian diplomat serving in London— Eugene Ivanov.

Miss Keeler produced a letter Mr. had written to her in 1961.

Now that Mr. Profumo is the cen[tre] grave political scandal, and now he fessed to the impropriety of his as[sociation] with Miss Keeler, THAT LETTER IS DUCED ON THIS PAGE TODAY.

But for two very sound reasons the the Sunday Pictorial decided not to pu letter or to publish Christine Keeler's

● The Editor was not satisfied t[hat] letter constituted evidence of any tial nature. It was effusive but not c[on]

● Publication of the letter might hav[e] the public career of a Minister dence" from a young woman who clea[r] not have produced the letter if Mr. P[rofumo] interests were uppermost in her consi[deration]

Not Disclosed

The existence of the letter was not to the public. Miss Christine Keele[r] was not published.

Dr. Stephen Ward, who was arreste[d] Scotland Yard officers yesterday, of write a story himself, and his article— "My Friendship with Christine"—app the Sunday Pictorial on March 17.

Dr. Ward referred to Mr. Profum[o] published on this page today, in an with the Daily Telegraph two days a[go]

THE FACTS ARE:

● Miss Keeler herself had not asked return of Mr. Profumo's letter.

● The letter was never discussed du Ward's negotiations with the

Turn to Back

What the letter said:

9-8-61

Darling,

In great haste and because I can get no reply from your phone—

Alas something's blown up tomorrow night and I can't therefore make it. I'm terribly sorry especially as I leave the next day for various trips and then a holiday so

won't be able to see you again u[ntil] some time in September. Blas[t it.] Please take great care of you[rself] and don't run away.

Love

I'm writing this 'cos I k[now] you're off for the day tomorrow I want you to know before you if I still can't reach you by pho[ne]

CONTENTS

CIRCUMSTANCES LEADING TO THE RESIGNATION OF MR J.D. PROFUMO

The principal persons

The story must start with Stephen Ward, aged fifty. The son of a clergyman, by profession he was an osteopath with consulting rooms at 38 Devonshire Street W1. His skill was very considerable and he included among his patients many well-known people. He was also an accomplished portrait artist. His sitters included people of much eminence. He had a quick and easy manner of conversation which attracted some but repelled others. It pleased him to meet people in high places, and he was prone to exaggerate the nature of acquaintanceships with them. He would speak of many of them as if they were great friends when, more often than not, he had only treated them as patients or drawn their portraits.

Yet he was at the same time utterly immoral. He had a small house or flat in London at 17 Wimpole Mews W1 and a country cottage on the Cliveden Estate next to the River Thames. He used to pick up pretty girls at the age of sixteen or seventeen, often from night clubs, and induce them to come and stay with him at his house in London. He used to take these girls down at week-ends to his cottage. He seduced many of these himself. He also procured them to be mistresses for his influential friends. He did not confine his attention to promiscuity. He catered also for those of his friends who had perverted tastes. There is evidence that he was ready to arrange for whipping and other sadistic perform-ances. He kept collections of pornographic photographs. He attended parties where there were sexual orgies of a revolting nature. In money matters he was improvident. He did not keep a banking account. He got a firm of solicitors to keep a sort of banking account for him, paying in cheques occasionally to them and getting them to pay his rent. More often he cashed cheques

Dr Stephen Ward, society osteopath, July 1963

through other people; or paid his bills with incoming cheques. He had many cash transactions which left no trace.

Finally, he admired the Soviet regime and sympathized with the communists. He used to advocate their cause in conversation with his patients, so much so that several became suspicious of him. He became very friendly with a Russian, Captain Eugene Ivanov. To him I now turn.

Captain Eugene Ivanov was an assistant Russian Naval Attaché at the Russian Embassy in London. As such his role would be diplomatic only. He came to this country on 27 March 1960. But the Security Service discovered that he was also a Russian Intelligence Officer. He had qualities not normally found in a Russian officer in this country. His English was reasonably good and he was able to converse easily. He drank, however, a good deal and was something of a ladies' man. He was keen to meet people in this country. He was very impressed by persons of title, particularly peers of the realm. He lost no opportunity of advocating the Russian viewpoint. He was, according to Stephen Ward, 'an absolutely dedicated Communist and also a nice person'. And he was quite open about his position. From the start he would tell his hearers, 'Anything you say goes back to Moscow. Look out what you say.'

Stephen Ward and Captain Ivanov became great friends. Captain Ivanov was often down at the cottage at Cliveden at weekends. He visited Stephen Ward's house in London. They met in restaurants. They often played bridge together. Stephen Ward introduced him to many of his friends, both those of high rank and also the girls. And Stephen Ward lost no opportunity of helping him, as the events show.

It has been suggested to me that Ivanov filled a new role in Russian technique. It was to divide the United Kingdom from the United States by these devious means. If Ministers or prominent people can be placed in compromising situations, or made the

subject of damaging rumour, or the Security Service can be made to appear incompetent, it may weaken the confidence of the United States in our integrity and reliability. So a man like Captain Ivanov may take every opportunity of getting to know Ministers or prominent people – not so much to obtain information from them (though this would be a useful by-product) – but so as to work towards destroying confidence. If this were the object of Captain Ivanov with Stephen Ward as his tool he succeeded only too well.

Christine Keeler is a girl, now aged 21, whose home is at Wraysbury. She left home at the age of 16 and went to London. She was soon employed at the Murray Cabaret Club as a show-girl, which involved, as she put it, just walking around with no clothes on. She had only been at the Cabaret Club a short time when Stephen Ward came there and they danced together. Thereafter he often telephoned her and took her out. After a very few days he asked her to go and live with him. She went. She ran away from him many times but she always went back. He seemed to control her. She lived with him at 17 Wimpole Mews, from about June 1961 to March 1962. He took her to his country cottage at Cliveden and he introduced her to many men, sometimes men of rank and position, with whom she had sexual intercourse. (A jury has since found him guilty on a charge of living on the earnings of her prostitution.) She had undoubted physical attractions. Later on he introduced her also to the drug Indian hemp and she became addicted to it. She met coloured men who trafficked in it and she went to live with them.

Mr Profumo was Secretary of State for War from July 1960 to June 1963. He is now aged 48. He had a fine war record and rose to the rank of brigadier. He entered Parliament in 1940 but lost his seat in 1945. In 1950 he came back as the Member for the Stratford Division of Warwickshire. He has a distinguished record of service

John Profumo and his wife, the former actress Valerie Hobson, before the scandal which destroyed his career, October 1959

to the country. He was Joint Parliamentary Secretary to the Ministry of Transport and Civil Aviation (1952), Parliamentary Under-Secretary of State for the Colonies (1957) and Under-Secretary and later Minister of State, Foreign Office (1958); and in 1960 he became Secretary of State for War. No one can doubt that a man with such a record was entitled to the confidence of his colleagues and of the country; and it should not be assumed by anyone that he would give away secret information. Whatever indiscretions he may have committed, and whatever falsehoods he may have told, no one who has given evidence before me has doubted his loyalty. In particular there was no reason for the Security Service to suspect it.

Mr Profumo married in 1954 Miss Valerie Hobson, a talented actress, and her support of him over their difficult days is one of the most redeeming features of the events I have to describe.

Lord Astor succeeded his father in 1952 and inherited the estate at Cliveden. He had previously taken an active part in politics but since that time he has devoted himself to his private affairs and to charities in which he is interested. He has done valuable work for hospitals, particularly the Canadian Red Cross Memorial Hospital at Cliveden. He has done a great deal for refugees, and has been all over the world on their behalf. He has provided a large sum as a Foundation for scientific and other studies. He has played an important part in many educational and social charities. He has also important business interests. He inherited a famous stud of race-horses, which he manages himself, and also a farm of 250 acres.

Cliveden is one of the great houses of the country. It is owned by the National Trust but the present Lord Astor is the tenant. He has upheld its tradition of hospitality. He has guests staying most weekends and often friends for meals. They include the names of some of the most distinguished and respected people in the land.

Lord Astor got to know Stephen Ward in 1950 when he went to

him as a patient after a fall at hunting. Stephen Ward treated him well and cured him. Ever since that time Lord Astor has sent him many of his friends as patients.

In 1956 Lord Astor let Stephen Ward a cottage on the Cliveden Estate. The cottage was down by the river, while the big house is on top of the hill. To get from the cottage to the house it is a quarter to half a mile's steep walk, or one mile by road. Stephen Ward used to come up at weekends and give osteopathic treatment to Lord Astor and to those of his guests who desired it. The account, including payment for the guests, was charged to Lord Astor. Stephen Ward often had visitors at this cottage. Usually they came for the day, and remained down at the cottage. When Stephen Ward went to the big house to give treatment he went by himself. On occasions, Lord Astor invited him to come up to Cliveden for lunch or for drinks.

Lord Astor had no sympathy with Stephen Ward's political views and made it clear to him. But at the pressing request of Stephen Ward, he did on occasions help him in approaching the Foreign Office (as will appear later), but not in any way sponsoring his views.

Lord Astor has helped Stephen Ward with money from time to time. In 1952, when Stephen Ward was starting but not yet established in practice, Lord Astor lent him £1,250, which Stephen Ward repaid over the succeeding years by professional services. And Lord Astor has on occasion advanced sums to him since, on the understanding that it was an advance to be repaid by expenses of treatment. In May 1963 Stephen Ward opened a banking account and Lord Astor guaranteed an overdraft up to £1,500. This was because Stephen Ward anticipated legal expenses and also desired to acquire premises for an office and residence. All the receipts from his practice and elsewhere were to go towards repayment.

The Cliveden weekend and its sequel

Stephen Ward often expressed a wish to go to Moscow. He wanted to draw pictures of the personalities there, particularly Mr Khrushchev. He told this to the Editor of a newspaper who was a patient of his. The Editor happened to have met Captain Ivanov: and invited Stephen Ward to lunch and meet him. This was on 20th January 1961. Stephen Ward took an immediate liking to Captain Ivanov. He began to enlist Ivanov's help to arrange sittings with Mr Khrushchev. The Security Service got to know of their friendship and on 8th June 1961 saw Stephen Ward about it. A few weeks later came the Cliveden weekend.

The weekend of Saturday, 8th July 1961 to Sunday, 9th July 1961 is of critical importance. Lord and Lady Astor had a large party of distinguished visitors to their great house at Cliveden. They included Mr Profumo, the Secretary of State for War, and his wife, Mrs Profumo, who stayed the weekend. Other visitors came to meals but did not stay the night. Stephen Ward entertained some young girls at his cottage. One of these was Christine Keeler, who was then living with him. Captain Ivanov came down on the Sunday. There is a fine swimming pool in the grounds at Cliveden near the main house, and Lord Astor, on occasions, allowed Stephen Ward to use it with his friends so long as it did not clash with his own use of it.

On the Saturday, after nightfall, Stephen Ward and some of the girls were bathing in the swimming pool when one of them, Christine Keeler, whilst she was in the water, took off her bathing costume, threw it on the bank, and bathed naked. Soon afterwards Lord Astor and a party of his visitors walked down after dinner to the swimming pool to watch the bathing. Lord Astor and Mr

Balcony and gardens of Cliveden, Taplow, England

Profumo walked ahead of Lady Astor, Mrs Profumo and the others. Christine Keeler rushed to get her swimming costume. Stephen Ward threw it on one side so that she could not get it at once and Christine seized a towel to hide herself. Lord Astor and Mr Profumo arrived at this moment, and it was all treated as a piece of fun – it was over in a few minutes, for the ladies saw nothing indecent at all. Stephen Ward and the girls afterwards got dressed and went up to the house and joined the party for a little while.

On the Sunday, after lunch, Stephen Ward and the girls and Captain Ivanov went to the swimming pool. Later Lord Astor and others of his party came down to swim too. There was a light-hearted, frolicsome bathing party, where everyone was in bathing costumes and nothing indecent took place at all. Photographs were taken by Mr Profumo and others. They showed, of course, that Mr Profumo was there with some of the girls but nothing improper whatever.

Captain Ivanov left Cliveden in the early evening and took Christine Keeler back with him to town. They went to Stephen Ward's house and there drank a good deal and there were perhaps some kind of sexual relations. Captain Ivanov left the house before Stephen Ward himself got back at midnight. But Captain Ivanov never became the lover of Christine.

It is apparent that during this weekend Mr Profumo was much attracted by Christine Keeler and determined to see her again, if he could. This was, of course, easy, through Stephen Ward. In the next few days and weeks Mr Profumo made assignations with Christine Keeler. He visited her at Stephen Ward's house and had sexual intercourse with her there. Sometimes he called at a time when Stephen Ward or someone else was there. He would then take her for a drive until the coast was clear. On one occasion he did not use his own car because his wife had it in the country. He used a car belonging to a Minister which had a mascot on it. He drove her to see Whitehall and Downing Street, also Regent's Park. Mr Profumo wrote two or three notes to Christine Keeler and gave her one or two presents such as perfume and a cigarette lighter. She said her parents were badly off and he gave her £20 for them, realizing that this was a polite way on her part of asking for money for her services. In August 1961, whilst his wife was in the Isle of Wight, he took Christine Keeler to his own house in Regent's Park. Altogether I am satisfied that his object in visiting her was simply because he was attracted by her and desired sexual intercourse with her.

It has been suggested that Captain Ivanov was her lover also. I do not think he was. The night of Sunday 9th July 1961 was an isolated occasion. I think that Captain Ivanov went to Stephen Ward's house for social entertainment and conversation, and not for sexual intercourse. I do not believe that Captain Ivanov and Mr Profumo ever met in Stephen Ward's house or in the doorway. They did no doubt narrowly miss one another on occasions: and this afforded Stephen Ward and Christine Keeler much amusement. (Later on a great deal has been made of this episode. It has been suggested that Captain Ivanov and Mr Profumo were sharing her services. I do not accept this suggestion.)

About this time, probably during the Cliveden weekend, Captain Ivanov told Stephen Ward that the Russians knew as a fact that the American Government had taken a decision to arm Western Germany with atomic weapons, and he asked Ward to find out through his influential friends when this decision was to be implemented. Without saying so in so many words, Captain Ivanov with some subtlety implied that if Stephen Ward supplied the answer his trip to Moscow would be facilitated.

One of the most critical points in my inquiry is this: Did Stephen Ward ask Christine Keeler to obtain from Mr Profumo information as to the time when the Americans were going to supply the atomic bomb to Germany? If he did ask her, it was probably at this time in July 1961: for it was the very thing that Captain Ivanov had asked Stephen Ward to find out from his influential friends. I am very dubious about her recollection about this. She has given several different versions of it and put it at different dates. (She once said it was at the time of the Cuban crisis in October 1962.*) The truth about it is, I think, this: There was a good deal of talk in her presence, between Stephen Ward and Captain Ivanov, about getting this information. And Stephen Ward may well have turned to her and said, 'You ought to ask Jack (Profumo) about it'. But I do not think it was said as seriously as it has since been reported. Stephen Ward said to me (and here I believed him):

> Quite honestly, nobody in their right senses would have asked somebody like Christine Keeler to obtain any information of that sort from Mr Profumo – he would have jumped out of his skin.

If said at all by Stephen Ward, it was, I believe, not said seriously expecting her to act on it. I am quite satisfied that she never acted on it. She told me, and I believed her, that she never asked Mr Profumo for the information. Mr Profumo was also clear that she never asked him, and I am quite sure that he would not have told her if she had asked him. (Later on a great deal has been made of this episode. I think the importance of it has been greatly exaggerated.)

On the 31st July 1961 the Head of the Security Service suggested to Sir Norman Brook (the then Secretary of the Cabinet, now Lord Normanbrook) that it might be useful for him to have a word with Mr Profumo about Stephen Ward and Captain Ivanov. (I will

---

* A time of acute international tension and political military confrontation between the USA and the USSR following the USA's discovery of Soviet nuclear missile sites in Cuba. Khrushchev agreed to dismantle the base in return for the withdrawal of US missiles from Turkey.

deal with the reasons for this later when I deal with the operation of the Security Service.) In accordance with this request, on 9th August 1961 Sir Norman Brook suggested to Mr Profumo that he should be careful in his dealings with Stephen Ward. He said there were indications that Stephen Ward might be interested in picking up scraps of information and passing them on to Captain Ivanov. Mr Profumo was grateful for the warning. He told Sir Norman that he met Captain Ivanov at the Cliveden weekend and then, after the encounter at Cliveden, he saw Captain Ivanov at a reception at the Soviet Embassy. On that occasion Captain Ivanov seemed to make a special point of being civil to him.

These were the only two occasions on which Mr Profumo had come across Captain Ivanov. On the other hand he was better acquainted with Stephen Ward. Mr Profumo went on to say that many people knew Stephen Ward and it might be helpful if warning were given to others too. He mentioned the name of another Cabinet Minister whom Sir Norman afterwards did warn. Sir Norman Brook referred rather delicately to another matter which had been suggested by the Head of the Security Service. Was it possible to do anything to persuade Ivanov to help us? But Mr Profumo thought he ought to keep well away from it.

It has been suggested that Sir Norman Brook went beyond his province at this point; and that he ought to have reported to the Prime Minister, and not taken it upon himself to speak to Mr Profumo. I think this criticism is based on a misapprehension. Neither the Security Service nor Sir Norman Brook had any doubts of Mr Profumo. They did not know that he was having an affair with Christine Keeler and had no reason to suspect it. I have seen a note made by Sir Norman Brook at the time of all that he was told by the Head of the Security Service. The main point being made by them was that Stephen Ward might be indiscreet and pass on bits of information to Captain Ivanov. It was therefore desirable to warn Mr Profumo of this possibility. Furthermore there was a thought that Captain Ivanov might be persuaded to defect. These seem to me to be matters which were very suitable for the Secretary of the Cabinet to mention to him, but hardly such as to need the intervention of the Prime Minister.

It was on Wednesday 9th August 1961 that Sir Norman Brook spoke to Mr Profumo. It made a considerable impression on him. Mr Profumo thought that the Security Service must have got knowledge of his affair with Christine Keeler, and that the real object of Sir Norman's call on him (though not expressed) was politely to indicate that his assignations with Christine Keeler should cease. It so happened that Mr Profumo had already arranged to see her the next night (Thursday, 10th August) but, as soon as Sir Norman left, he took steps to cancel the arrangement.

Mr Profumo wrote this letter to Christine Keeler:

9/8/61

Darling,

In great haste and because I can get no reply from your phone – Alas something's blown up tomorrow night and I can't therefore make it. I'm terribly sorry especially as I leave the next day for various trips and then a holiday so won't be able to see you again until some time in September. Blast it. Please take great care of yourself and don't run away.

Love J.

PS: I'm writing this 'cos I know you're off for the day tomorrow and I want you to know before you go if I still can't reach you by phone.

I am satisfied that that letter, if not the end, was the beginning of the end of the association between Mr Profumo and Christine Keeler. He may have seen her a few times more but that was all. It

Prime Minister Harold Macmillan at Euston Station, London, at the height of the Profumo scandal

meant also that he stopped seeing Stephen Ward. Sir Norman Brook's talk had had its effect on him. Mr Profumo only saw Stephen Ward again about the end of January 1963 when there was a fear that his association with Christine Keeler would be made public. It has been said in some quarters that Mr Profumo went on visiting Christine Keeler in 1962 when she was in Dolphin Square. 'Lucky' Gordon gave evidence before me to this effect. So did a man called Hogan. They said they knew it was Mr Profumo by having seen his photographs in the newspapers. I found myself unable to accept their evidence. Mr Hogan had given a story to a newspaper that he was 'butler' to Christine Keeler and took up coffee on two occasions to Mr Profumo and Christine Keeler in bed. He told me that he had signed a contract for £600 for this story to be split between him and two freelance reporters. But he was not a butler at all. He was a carpet cleaner.

I have found it difficult to fix a definite date for the end of the association. When Mr Profumo was seen by the Chief Whip on 4th February 1963 he said it had 'all taken place between July and December of 1961', and in his statement in the House of Commons on 22nd March 1963 he said, 'I last saw Miss Keeler in December 1961, and I have not seen her since'. Christine Keeler herself, in her statement to the Press on 26th March 1963. adopted this date, evidently following him. I have heard their evidence on this point. Mr Profumo is sure that he brought it to an end when Sir Norman Brook gave him the warning, and he wrote the letter to her the self-same day. The mistake about the date was because he remembered Sir Norman Brook saying, 'I thought I should see you before we go away for the recess', and he thought it wa the December recess (not having the letter or date before him) but later on, when he got the date, he realized it was in fact the August recess. Whatever be the truth about this, I am quite satisfied the association did not last very long. It certainly ended by December 1961.

Aloysius 'Lucky' Gordon arriving at the Old Bailey, December 1963

Stephen Ward helping the Russians

After August 1961 Stephen Ward saw little or nothing of Mr Profumo. But he continued very friendly with Captain Ivanov and it is plain that Captain Ivanov was continually asking Stephen Ward questions about the general political intentions of the British, and that Stephen Ward did his best to get all the information he could for Ivanov. He sought help from influential friends, particularly Lord Astor and Sir Godfrey Nicholson, MP.

One thing he did was to get Lord Astor to write to the Foreign Office on 2nd September 1961. In this letter Lord Astor said he had a friend called Stephen Ward, who had become a friend of Captain Ivanov, and suggested that if the Foreign Office wished to ensure at any particular moment that the Russian Embassy was absolutely correctly informed as to Western intentions, Stephen Ward would be useful. Stephen Ward could pass on the information himself or could very easily arrange for Captain Ivanov to meet anyone. In consequence of this letter, on 18th September 1961 the Foreign Office interviewed Stephen Ward. He gave a long account of his political views and said that he was anxious to turn his friendship with Captain Ivanov to useful account. He was told quite plainly that the Foreign Office would not wish to avail themselves of his services.

The next thing he did was to get Sir Godfrey Nicholson, MP, to meet Captain Ivanov. (Sir Godfrey knew Stephen Ward well and had been a patient of his for many years – and had recommended him to many others. Sir Godfrey is, of course, a most loyal Englishman.)

Stephen Ward sought to use Sir Godfrey as a means of getting information for Captain Ivanov from the Foreign Office about British intentions over disarmament and over Berlin. Sir Godfrey did see the Foreign Office, and indeed the Foreign Secretary; and he wrote three letters to Captain Ivanov about the Berlin matter and the Oder–Neisse line. But he was careful to submit the draft of these letters to the Foreign Office and get them approved before he sent them. (Lord Home went so far as to warn Sir Godfrey not to see Captain Ivanov, but Sir Godfrey felt that as a Member of Parliament he must be free to talk to him.) Stephen Ward did not rest there. He wanted to meet Sir Harold Caccia, the Permanent Under-Secretary of State at the Foreign Office, and on 5th April 1962 Sir Godfrey arranged a luncheon where Stephen Ward met Sir Harold. Stephen Ward offered to put Sir Harold in direct touch with Captain Ivanov but Sir Harold declined the offer. The Foreign Office was under no illusions as to Stephen Ward.

In late October 1962 there was the Cuban crisis, when the Russian ships were heading towards Cuba with nuclear weapons. Stephen Ward played a very active part at this juncture. He seems to have been acting on the suggestion of Captain Ivanov. Stephen Ward's point was that the Soviet Government looked to the United Kingdom as the only hope of mediation in this crisis and that the United Kingdom should call a summit conference to resolve it. Stephen Ward, on 24th October 1962, telephoned the Foreign Office and said that Lord Astor had recommended him to contact Sir Harold Caccia; and he put forward the suggestion of a summit conference. On 25th October 1962 he got Sir Godfrey Nicholson to meet Captain Ivanov and then, at Captain Ivanov's request, to go to the Foreign Office with the same proposal. Stephen Ward afterwards himself telephoned to the Foreign Office about it. On the same day he got Lord Astor to speak to Lord Arran. Lord Astor told Lord Arran that there was a Russian official (no doubt it was Captain Ivanov) who was seeking to pass information of an urgent nature to the British Government. Two days later, on 27th October 1962, Stephen Ward took Captain Ivanov to Lord Arran's house. Captain Ivanov told Lord Arran that he wished to convey a message to the British Government by indirect means asking them to call a summit conference in London forthwith. He maintained that Mr Khrushchev would accept the invitation with alacrity, and thus the United Kingdom would break the deadlock. Lord Arran suspected that this was an attempt to drive a wedge between the United Kingdom and the Americans. He reported it both to the Foreign Office and to Admiralty House.

All these efforts by Stephen Ward failed. It so happened that on Sunday, 28th October 1962 there was another party at Cliveden. Lord Astor's guests included Lord Arran. Stephen Ward and Captain Ivanov came up to the house. While they were there news came through over the broadcast that the Russian ships had turned back from Cuba. Captain Ivanov could not, indeed did not, conceal his anger and discomfiture. All the guests noticed it.

Looking back on the incident, Stephen Ward told me that he felt at the time that he was doing something momentous, but afterwards he realized that it was of little real significance. I accept that Stephen Ward's activities, although misconceived and mis-directed, were not deliberately mischievous, and I am goad to say that over this critical period the efforts of Stephen Ward and Captain Ivanov did not have the slightest effect on any of the people whom they approached – except to make everyone more suspicious of them than ever.

Shortly after the Cuban crisis, on 31st October 1962, there was an incident which will illustrate the way in which Stephen Ward was apt to drop names of well-known people which led to unfounded rumours about them. In the evening of 31st October 1962 Mr William S. Shepherd, MP, went to Stephen Ward's house. He found, as he says, Captain Ivanov there, Christine Keeler, and also Marilyn Rice-Davies. (She was another of the girls whom Stephen Ward found and she was currently living in his house.) They did not know that Mr Shepherd was a Member of

Parliament. The conversation turned to the Cuban crisis. Mr Shepherd said it was a victory for the Americans. Captain Ivanov became very angry. When Mr Shepherd got up to go Stephen Ward said, referring to Captain Ivanov and himself, 'we must go too. We are going to have dinner with Iain Macleod' – which Mr Shepherd thought was an extraordinary thing. This was a typical distortion of the truth by Stephen Ward. They were not going to have dinner with Mr Macleod at all.

The fact was that on 31st October 1962 there was a party at Mr and Mrs Macleod's flat at 36 Sloane Court West. Stephen Ward and Captain Ivanov simply 'gate-crashed'. There is no other word for it. It was a party for young people all aged about 18 or 19. On the morning of the party one of the young invited guests (who evidently knew Stephen Ward) telephoned and asked if he could bring along Stephen Ward and a friend of his. He had evidently been put up to this by Stephen Ward. The Macleods did not know anything about Stephen Ward but assumed it was all right and said 'Yes'. Stephen Ward came rather late to the party and brought with him Captain Ivanov. They did not stay long. They did not meet Mr Iain Macleod at all. He was in the House of Commons and did not attend the party. Mrs Macleod came in towards the end of the party and saw these two men who were much older than anyone else. She spoke a word or two to Stephen Ward (whom she did not know) but did not speak to Captain Ivanov. The two only stayed a few minutes and then left. None of the Macleod family have seen or heard of either of them again. Mrs Macleod told Mr Macleod next day about it.

Mr Shepherd was so suspicious that, a day or two later, he took the opportunity of mentioning the matter to Mr Macleod. He said that Stephen Ward had been giving the impression that he had been invited to Mr Macleod's flat and knew him. Mr Macleod explained to Mr Shepherd just what had happened and spoke to the Foreign Secretary (Lord Home) about it and wrote a letter putting it on record. The Foreign Secretary of course knew a good deal about Stephen Ward by this time.

It is quite obvious now that Stephen Ward was seeking an opportunity for Captain Ivanov to meet Mr Macleod and others, to glean, I suppose, any information he could, for the Russians. It is equally obvious that he got nothing.

On the 7th November 1962 Ward followed up his activities during the Cuban crisis by reporting them to Mr Harold Wilson, MP, the Leader of the Opposition. He wrote saying that on Friday, 26th October, an offer was made by the Russians to the Foreign Office for a summit conference. 'I can vouch for the authenticity of this', he said, 'since I was the intermediary.' Mr Wilson did not think this letter at the time to be of any account and sent a non-committal reply.

On 26th December 1962 Lord and Lady Ednam held a dinner party to which a high official of the Foreign Office and his wife were invited. Stephen Ward and Captain Ivanov were also present at the dinner party. They brought up the Nassau Conference[*] and the possibility of Germany acquiring nuclear weapons. But the Foreign Office official gave nothing away.

Thus ends the known activities of Ward on behalf of the Russians. He was without doubt a Communist sympathizer, and so much under the influence of Ivanov that he was a potential danger. But this was known to the Security Service and they had passed it on to the people who mattered, particularly the Foreign Office, and any Ministers who might come into contact with him. I see no failure of the Security Service over this period. I will set out the details of their work later.

* December 1962. At which an agreement was made between UK Prime Minister Harold Macmillan and US President John F. Kennedy whereby the USA supplied Polaris missiles for British nuclear submarines.

The slashing and shooting

Whilst Stephen Ward was thus engaging himself busily during 1962 in aid of Ivanov and the Russians he had continued his vicious sexual activities. He wanted a coloured girl and got Christine Keeler to get him one. In October 1961 he took her to the Rio Café in the Westbourne Park Road. There were coloured people there. Some were smokers of 'reefers', that is, drugged cigarettes, and were engaged in trafficking in Indian hemp. She here met 'Lucky' Gordon for the first time. She asked him, 'Can I have some weed?' and he let her have 10 shillings' worth. He wanted to see her again. She said, 'I can only see you if you bring your sister for my brother' (meaning a coloured girl for Stephen Ward). And thus she started her association with coloured men. Some time later she left Stephen Ward and went to live with this man 'Lucky' Gordon. Later she took up a similar association with another one called John Edgecombe. Each of these seems to have considered her to be his property. This led to extreme jealousy which resulted in violence.

On 27th–28th October 1962 Christine Keeler was with Edgecombe at an 'All Nighters Club' in Wardour Street, W1, in the early hours of the morning. 'Lucky' Gordon arrived and there was an argument between the two men about her. It flared up into an affray in which 'Lucky' Gordon's face was slashed, necessitating 17 stitches. The police sought to arrest John Edgecombe and charge him with an assault, but he disappeared. He went to Brentford, and Christine Keeler went to live with him there. Meanwhile Stephen Ward got Marilyn Rice-Davies to live with him in 17 Wimpole Mews.

Early in December 1962 Christine Keeler left John Edgecombe. He determined to get her back if he could. On 14th December

1962 she went to 17 Wimpole Mews, where she was visiting Marilyn Rice-Davies. At about 1 p.m. John Edgecombe arrived in a mini-cab. He told the driver to wait. Marilyn Rice-Davies looked out of the window. John Edgecombe asked for Christine Keeler. Marilyn Rice-Davies said she was not in. He kept on ringing the bell. After a while Christine Keeler put her head out of the window and told him to go away. He charged at the door to try and break it open. It withstood the charge. He then pulled out an automatic pistol and fired shots at the lock on the front door. Three or four shots. Once more the window upstairs was opened. He pointed the pistol in that direction and shot again. Only a shot or two this time, for he had come to the end of his ammunition. He went back to the mini-cab and got the driver of the mini-cab to drive him back to Brentford. The police caught up with him there and he was arrested. He was charged, not only with this shooting but also with the slashing of 'Lucky' Gordon on 27th October 1962.

Meanwhile, however, the shooting had attracted the attention of the neighbourhood. One of the girls had telephoned Stephen Ward at his surgery in nearby Devonshire Street and gave him a running commentary of what was happening. He heard the shooting over the telephone. He telephoned the police. Wireless messages were sent out from the police station but the newspapermen arrived in the Mews before the police. The Mews was filled with Press and police. The police took the girls to the police station and took statements from them as to the shooting. The station was besieged by the Press but eventually the girls got away and went to a flat which Christine Keeler had taken at 63 Great Cumberland Place.

After they got back to the flat Christine Keeler telephoned Mr Michael Eddowes. (He was a retired solicitor who was a friend and patient of Stephen Ward. He had befriended Christine Keeler and had taken her to see her mother once or twice.) She told him of the shooting. He already knew from Stephen Ward something of her relations with Captain Ivanov and Mr Profumo, and he asked her about them. He was most interested and subsequently noted it down in writing, and in March he reported it to the police. He followed it up by employing an ex-member of the Metropolitan Police to act as detective on his behalf to gather information.

It was quite plain that Christine Keeler would be an important witness in the case against John Edgecombe, both with regard to the slashing of 'Lucky' Gordon and also the shooting. John Edgecombe was remanded in custody from time to time and the evidence was not taken by the magistrate until the 16th and 17th January 1963. Christine Keeler attended the magistrate's hearings quite voluntarily and gave evidence for the prosecution. John Edgecombe was committed for trial at the Old Bailey. His trial was expected to be early in February.

On Sunday 3rd February 1963 the *News of the World* published a large picture of Christine Keeler, in a seductive pose, with nothing on except the slightest of swimming garbs, and the words alongside: 'Model in shots case. Attractive Christine Keeler, a 20-year-old London model, features in a case at the Old Bailey this week in which a man is accused of shooting at her with intent to murder. He is a 30-year-old West Indian, John Edgecombe, of Brentford, Middlesex.' I mention this photograph because most people seeing it would readily infer the avocation of Christine Keeler.

The trial of John Edgecombe did not, however, take place that week. The driver of the mini-cab was taken ill. On Friday, 8th February 1963 a medical certificate was received by the police that he was unable to attend the Court, and it was decided to apply for an adjournment. The case came on for trial on 14th March 1963 but by that time Christine Keeler had disappeared. Meanwhile, however, much had happened. The shooting had been given much notice in the newspapers. Many saw that a story might emerge of much interest. It did.

Christine tells her story

On the very night of the shooting Christine Keeler told something of her story to Mr Michael Eddowes, but it does not seem to have gained publicity through him. She told it later in circles where it was soon taken up.

About nine days after the shooting, on 23rd December 1962, there was a party in a girl's flat in Rossmore Court. Christine Keeler went there with Paul Mann. John Lewis, formerly a Member of Parliament, went to the party with a friend. In the course of conversation the shooting was discussed. Stephen Ward's name was mentioned, and at once old memories revived. John Lewis and Stephen Ward had been engaged actively in litigation in 1954 and 1955 and there was no love lost between them. Christine Keeler said how fearful she was of being called as a witness. John Lewis said she must be represented in court and recommended her to a solicitor. He was most interested in her story and over the next two or three weeks made a point of seeing her and obtaining more details. She told him of her affair with Mr Profumo and of the letters he had written to her. She also told him that Stephen Ward asked her to obtain information from Mr Profumo as to the date when the Americans would deliver atom bombs to Germany.

John Lewis was at once alive to the importance of the matter from the security point of view. He told Mr George Wigg, MP, about it. And from that time onwards he kept Mr Wigg fully informed of every development. They had conversations almost daily. John Lewis was so interested that he, in March 1963, got his own agent to investigate in the person of a journalist who spent much of his time in Stephen Ward's flat.

Next on the scene (they had been hovering near all the time) came the Press. Christine Keeler told her story to Paul Mann. Now Paul Mann was a young man aged 26. He had been at the Cliveden weekend. He was at this time (December 1962) in a shirt business in Manchester, but often came down to London at week-ends. He also seems to have friends in journalism. He was friendly both with Stephen Ward and Christine Keeler. Another acquaintance of Christine Keeler's was a woman called Nina Gadd who was a freelance journalist. It appears to have been indirectly through these two that her story achieved notice. They advised her that there were newspapers who would buy it. Only two possible buyers were mentioned to her: the *News of the World* and the *Sunday Pictorial*. She got in touch with both and tried to see who would pay her most.

Christine played off one against the other. When the *Sunday Pictorial* offered her £1,000, she went straight to the *News of the World* and asked them to increase it. Their representative said, 'I will see you to the devil. I will not join in any Dutch auction.' So the *Sunday Pictorial* succeeded. On 22nd January 1963 she went to the office of the *Sunday Pictorial* and signed a conditional contract to sell them her story for £1,000, of which £200 was to be paid down and the balance of £800 on completion. She outlined her story and gave it colour by relating her double life – with rich men in high places and coloured men in low. She told them of her relations with Mr Profumo and with Captain Ivanov. She produced Mr Profumo's letter of 9th August 1961 (the 'Darling' letter), in proof that she was telling the truth. The newspaper had it photographed and put it in the safe.

Over the next few days the newspapermen took down her story in detail and she then told the reporters (what she had not told them at first) that Stephen Ward had asked her to obtain from Mr Profumo information as to when the Americans were going to give

Christine Keeler arriving at court, October 1963

nuclear weapons to Germany. The newspaper reporters saw how greatly the 'spy' interest heightened the story.

The reporters of the *Sunday Pictorial* prepared a proof of her story. She signed every page as correct on 8th February 1963. It is the first signed statement she gave to anyone. (The police did not get a signed statement until 4th April 1963.) It is on that account instructive to see how she put it. It was in fact never published, but this is how it ran:

'Men are such fools. But I like them. I have always liked them.

Unfortunately, the combination of these things has led me into a lot of trouble and may even have risked the security of this country. It certainly could have been harmful to the country.

You see, one man who was foolish enough and irresponsible enough to have an affair with me was a Cabinet Minister, a member of Her Majesty's Government.

And at the same time I was having an affair with another man – a Russian diplomat.

If that Russian or anyone else had placed a tape recorder or cine camera or both in some hidden place in my bedroom, it would have been very embarrassing for the Minister, to say the least.

In fact, it would have left him open to the worst possible kind of blackmail – the blackmail of a spy.

I am not suggesting that he really would have given up State secrets to avoid a scandal. He might have been tough and refused.

But I do believe that any man in his position – particularly a married man – is both unwise and irresponsible to have an affair with some unknown girl like me.

More especially so in this case because this Minister has such knowledge of the military affairs of the Western world that he would be one of the most valuable men in the world for the Russians to have had in their power.

He is, in fact, the Secretary of State for War, Mr John Profumo.

I believe now that a man in his position should not indulge in pastimes like me. I suppose even Cabinet Ministers are only human, but I think they should curb their feelings when they take on the job.

One might think that as a politician he would have been particularly discreet in the affair. John Profumo was not. It is true he did not take me out much, but he did take me to his own home while his wife was away. And he did write letters to me.

One might also think that those responsible for State security would keep some sort of watch on men who hold as many secrets as he holds.

Yet if that happened he would never have been able to come and see me at the flat where I was being visited by the Russian.

And, believe me, the Russian was a man who would be very much aware of the value of the secrets which Profumo knew. He was not a civilian.

He was, in fact, a naval captain, Captain Eugene Ivanov.

Of course, at the time I did not realize the sinister implications behind my two affairs. I was only 18 and knew nothing of politics or international matters. I was not interested.

I did not realize then that blackmail is one of the Russians' favourite weapons when they are trying to recruit traitors or discover secret information.

I am sure that Jack Profumo would not have allowed his harmless affair with me to be used as a lever to prise secrets from him. But a weaker man in his position might have allowed it to happen .

At the time, however, I saw no danger in the situation. It just seemed funny to me that I should be seeing the two men, sometimes on the same day. One might leave my flat only a few minutes before the other arrived.

I did find it worrying when someone asked me to try to get from Profumo the answer to a certain question.

That question was: 'When, if ever, are the Americans going to give nuclear weapons to Germany?'

I am not prepared to say in public who asked me to find out the answer to that question. I am prepared to give it to the security officials. In fact, I believe now that I have a duty to do so.

On 26th January 1963 Detective-Sergeant Burrows of the Marylebone Police Station called on Christine Keeler to serve her with notice to attend the trial of John Edgecombe. It was only four days after she had signed her conditional contract with the *Sunday Pictorial*. She then told the Detective-Sergeant in brief outline the self-same story as she told the newspaper. This needs separate treatment and I will deal with it later.

By the end of January 1963, therefore, Christine Keeler had told her story to these people:

(1) Mr John Lewis and through him Mr George Wigg, MP

(2) The newspapers, particularly the *News of the World* and the *Sunday Pictorial*

(3) The police through Detective-Sergeant Burrows

(4) The Security Service got to know of her story about this time too.

Very shortly afterwards it also came to the knowledge of those at Admiralty House. This I will relate later.

Stephen Ward did not know at first of all this activity by Christine Keeler. He had quarrelled with her for the time being and did not know that she had gone to the newspaper. He had been turned out of his house at 17 Wimpole Mews, because he could not pay the rent, and had gone to a flat in Bryanston Mews formerly belonging to Peter Rachman. On 16th January 1963 he told a journalist all he knew about the shooting and said he had succeeded in keeping out of it and hoped the whole thing would blow over. But it did not. On 18th January 1963 he saw Captain

Ivanov, and it may be presumed that Captain Ivanov took alarm. It seems as if it was what is called a 'tip-off'. Captain Ivanov left England on 29th January 1963, much earlier than expected.

The crisis broke upon Stephen Ward on 26th January 1963 when a journalist went to see him and told him that he had been in contact with the girls and 'they are now with the *Sunday Pictorial*'. This was the signal for intensive activity by Stephen Ward. He did all he could to stop the publication. On Sunday, 27th January he went to the private house of his Counsel (Mr Rees-Davies, MP) and had some discussion with him.

On Monday, 28th January he telephoned to Lord Astor and asked him to meet him on a very, very urgent matter at the chambers of his Counsel; and both he and Lord Astor went to Counsel's chambers. Lord Astor did not stay long but arranged to instruct his own solicitor that afternoon (which he did). Stephen Ward stayed and told the problem to his Counsel: namely, that the trial of John Edgecombe was expected the next week; that Christine Keeler was to be called as a witness and might bring into her evidence the names of Stephen Ward and Mr Profumo; and that she had sold her story to the *Sunday Pictorial* and it might appear as soon as the trial was concluded. Stephen Ward's Counsel went to see the Solicitor-General and told him. The Solicitor-General passed it on to the Attorney-General. The Attorney-General wrote a note to Mr Profumo and asked him to come and see him.

Meanwhile, in the afternoon of the same day, Lord Astor saw his solicitor, and at 5.30 p.m. Lord Astor went to see Mr Profumo and told him of the danger. Mr Profumo at once got into touch with the Head of the Security Service and asked him to come and see him. The Head of the Security Service got the impression that Mr Profumo hoped he would get a D-notice[*] issued or something

[*] A notice officially sent to newspapers, etc., asking them not to publish certain information (D for defence).

to stop publication – but his hopes were in vain.

Over the next few days there was much going on – so much so that I must divide it into sections so as to show what was done by the police, the lawyers, and the Ministers of the Crown. But there were also two meetings of the principals. Mr Profumo wanted to know more about it all. He and Stephen Ward had lunch together with Lord Astor in Lord Astor's London house. Then Mr Profumo wanted 'to get a bit more out of Ward' and he met him at the Dorchester Hotel. Stephen Ward told him the newspaper had a letter which started 'Darling' and ended 'Love J'.

Stephen Ward with Mandy Rice-Davies, Penny Marshall and Christine Keeler, June 1963

The police are told

No one can understand the actions of the police in the Profumo affair unless it is realized that their primary task is to maintain law and order. In particular it is their duty to enforce the criminal law, and in this respect they are completely independent of the Home Office. It is no part of their duty to pry into the private lives of anyone, be it a Minister of the Crown or the humblest citizen. And if, in the course of their inquiries, they come across discreditable incidents in private lives (not amounting to a criminal offence) it is no part of their duty to report it to anyone. We are not yet a 'police state'. Even if they come across discreditable incidents in the life of a Minister, they are not to report it – save only if it appears that the security of the country may be endangered, when they should report it to the Security Service.

So much for what I may call the ordinary police force. There is also the 'Special Branch' of the Metropolitan Police. This was formed in 1886 to deal with Irish Republican activity. From that time it has developed so that its main activities are as follows:

- It is concerned with subversive or terrorist organizations. So one of its duties is to obtain information regarding them and pass it to the Security Service.
- It is also concerned with offences against the security of the State, such as treason, espionage, offences against the Official Secrets Act and the Public Order Act. If the Security Service, for instance, detect a spy, they collect the information and material about the case and then pass it to Special Branch. The Special Branch make any necessary searches or arrests and prepare the case for trial. Conversely, if Special Branch comes across material which points to a risk to national security, they

pass it to the Security Service for their information.

- It keeps watch on seaports and airports for criminals and other dangerous persons, makes inquiries into aliens, and so forth.

There is very close cooperation between the Special Branch and the Security Service. They work together in harmony and each has the fullest confidence in the other.

The various cases that figure in the Profumo affair illustrate very clearly the working of the ordinary police. In the Edgecombe case the ordinary police force handled it in the accustomed manner. On being informed of the shooting, they went at once to the scene, made investigations, then an arrest, afterwards took statements, and conducted the case right through to trial. In the Gordon case, too, as soon as the attack on Christine Keeler was reported, they acted in a similar manner. Likewise with the Ward case. This came to their notice through anonymous communications. They looked into it to see if there was anything to investigate, and, finding there was, they took statements which eventually disclosed a case against him, as a result of which they arrested him and conducted the case to trial.

The important point for present purposes is, however, this: In the course of the conduct of the Edgecombe case, the ordinary police officers came across information which might have a security significance and the question is whether it was handled properly by them, or by Special Branch or, later on, by the Security Service.

On Saturday, 26th January 1963 Detective-Sergeant Burrows of the Marylebone Police Station went to warn Christine Keeler and Marilyn Rice-Davies that they were required to attend at the Central Criminal Court at the trial of John Edgecombe. He served recognizance notices on them and then Christine Keeler voluntarily made a statement to him. (I give it from the note he made and in the very form he reported it to his superiors.)

She said that Doctor Ward was a procurer of women for gentlemen in high places and was sexually perverted; that he had a country cottage at Cliveden to which some of these women were taken to meet important men – the cottage was on the estate of Lord Astor; that he had introduced her to Mr John Profumo and that she had had an association with him; that Mr Profumo had written a number of letters to her on War Office notepaper and that she was still in possession of one of these letters which was being considered for publication in the *Sunday Pictorial,* to whom she had sold her life story for £1,000. She also said that on one occasion when she was going to meet Mr Profumo, Ward had asked her to discover from him the date on which certain atomic secrets were to be handed to West Germany by the Americans, and that this was at the time of the Cuban crisis. She also said that she had been introduced by Ward to the Naval Attaché of the Soviet Embassy and had met him on a number of occasions.

It is to be noticed that the statement of Christine Keeler contains in concise form the very gist of all the important matters: the procurement of women by Stephen Ward; the association of Mr Profumo with Christine Keeler; the request for information about atomic secrets; and the Ivanov relationship.

Detective-Sergeant Burrows reported it to his superior, Detective-Inspector Anning, who thought it was outside the field of crime but a matter for the Special Branch. So he telephoned to Detective-Inspector Morgan of Special Branch. He thought it of considerable security importance and felt that Christine Keeler should be seen by Special Branch. He arranged a meeting for Detective-Sergeant Burrows and himself to see her. Whilst he was making inquiries Christine Keeler told the police at Marylebone that she believed that Ward, in an endeavour to 'have her put away', was alleging that she was in possession of drugs. So it was thought advisable to have the assistance of an officer conversant with drugs. Arrangements were made for her to be seen at 3.30 p.m. on Friday, 1st February 1963 at her flat, No. 63 Great Cumberland Place. The officers who were to go were Detective-Sergeant Burrows (from Marylebone, who had seen her first), Detective-Inspector Morgan (of Special Branch because of the security interest) and Sergeant Howard of the Drug Squad (because of the drug suggestion).

It was most unfortunate that this meeting was never held. Christine Keeler was not seen at all by the police, or at any rate no statement was taken from her, from the day when she was seen by Detective-Sergeant Burrows on 26th January 1963 (which I have set out) until 4th April 1963 when inquiries were being made into the case against Stephen Ward.

The first question arises, therefore, why was the meeting not held on 1st February 1963? It was cancelled by order of the Commander of Special Branch. When the proposal was put before him on the morning of 1st February he decided that Special Branch should not take part in questioning Christine Keeler. He did this, he told me, because of the Press. He thought it inevitable that the Press would get to know that Christine Keeler had been seen by Special Branch and that would cause a lot of speculation. (He expected that Christine Keeler might well tell the Press herself that she had been seen by a Special Branch officer.) After discussion with his Deputy Commander, it was decided that Christine Keeler and Stephen Ward should be seen by officers of the Criminal Investigation Department, and that anything coming to light which was of interest to Special Branch should be brought to their notice. In consequence of this decision the Deputy Commander sent out a message cancelling the meeting arranged for the afternoon of Friday, 1st February 1963. No reason was given to the Marylebone officers. It was just cancelled. Detective-Sergeant Burrows accordingly telephoned Christine Keeler and

said he could not keep the appointment that afternoon, but would contact her again at some future date.

The second question arises why was Christine Keeler not seen at all at this time, not even by officers of the Criminal Investigation Department? This was the decision of a Chief Superintendent of the Department. The Deputy Commander of Special Branch told me that he made it clear that he wished Christine Keeler to be seen, but the Chief Superintendent of the Criminal Investigation Department told me that the message, as it reached him, was that Stephen Ward was to be seen; but nothing was said, he told me, about seeing Christine Keeler. There must have been some failure in coordination on this point. An appointment was made for Stephen Ward to be seen at Scotland Yard on Saturday, 2nd February 1963 by a Drug Squad official but Ward did not keep the appointment. In consequence on Monday, 4th February 1963 the Chief Superintendent decided not to make another appointment for him. In addition, on the same day he was asked by Special Branch whether he intended to have Christine Keeler seen, and he said he did not. This was, I think, an unfortunate decision: for it meant that she was not seen by any police officer at all at that time. There must have been another failure in coordination at this point. The decision was recorded in this minute by a Superintendent of Special Branch:

> The Chief Superintendent of Criminal Investigation does not propose making another appointment (for Ward), nor does he intend to have Miss Keeler seen. I told the Chief Superintendent that this was agreeable to Special Branch and we are not asking him to take any other action.

It is quite plain from this last sentence that the Superintendent of Special Branch did not regard it as important to see Christine

Keeler. He told me that he thought the crime interest was greater than any security risk. Accepting this view, nevertheless in view of Christine Keeler's statement to Detective-Sergeant Burrows it does appear that there was a security interest which should have been watched; and the Deputy Commander of Special Branch certainly intended her to be seen.

So much for Christine Keeler's statement. There was a statement by Stephen Ward at this time which was also of importance. On 4th February 1963 at 6.20 p.m. Stephen Ward himself telephoned to the Marylebone Lane Station and said that two photographs had been stolen from him. They were photographs taken at the swimming pool at Cliveden. One was taken by Mr Profumo and showed Stephen Ward with three girls, one of whom was Christine Keeler. Mr Profumo had written on it 'The new Cliveden Set, J.' The other, taken by someone else, showed Mr Profumo with two girls, one of whom was Christine Keeler. The Marylebone officers asked him to come to the station and he did so on 5th February 1963. Stephen Ward said he thought Paul Mann had stolen the photographs to sell. He also made this statement (from the note made by the officer as it was reported to his superior):

Dr Ward said that if this matter, including the association between Mr Profumo and Christine Keeler, became public, it might very well 'bring down' the Government. He also added that he had no personal liking for this Government but would not like to see it go out of office in this way. He also said that he was aware that Miss Keeler had sold her life story to the *Sunday Pictorial* newspaper and that a number of names would be mentioned. Ward also said that he was a close friend of the Naval Attaché of the Soviet Embassy, who frequently visited him and who was known in diplomatic circles as 'Foxface'. He produced a photograph which he said had been taken at an official Iron Curtain party and in it he appeared standing alongside 'Foxface'. He also said that he had mentioned the matter to a member of MI5.

It is to be noticed, too, that this statement of Stephen Ward's contained direct reference to two important matters – the association of Mr Profumo and Christine Keeler, and Stephen Ward's friendship for Ivanov.

We have at this point, therefore, two important statements to the police – one by Christine Keeler on 26th January 1963 and the other by Stephen Ward on 5th February 1963. The Marylebone officers embodied these in a written report dated 5th February 1963. (They were in the very terms I have quoted.) It was a pity that Christine Keeler had not been seen as intended, for if she had been seen, she might well have filled in much important detail (such as the description of Mr Profumo's house or the mascot on the car) which would have corroborated her story, and she might have thrown light on Stephen Ward's activities. It is a pity, too, that Stephen Ward was not seen by officers of Scotland Yard as intended, for a detailed statement from him at that time might have had important consequences.

Nevertheless the report of the Marylebone officer gave the gist of all the important matters. It may be asked, what did Special Branch do about this important report? They did the correct thing. They took it along to the Security Service. The report reached Special Branch on Thursday, 7th February 1963 and was considered by the Commander himself. He at once went and saw a senior officer of the Security Service. He took a copy of the report and left it with him. He asked two pertinent questions:

(a) Was there any security intelligence aspect which should influence Criminal Investigation Department action? The Security Officer said, No.

(b) Did any duty lie on Scotland Yard to ensure that Mr Profumo was aware of the likelihood of publicity? The Security Officer said that Mr Profumo was aware of it.

The Commander went back and drew up this minute:

> The facts given [in the report] were already known to [the Security Service] in broad outline. Their principal interest is, of course, the Russian diplomat, whose identity is known to them and in whose activities they are taking an interest. Officially they are not concerned with the Profumo aspect, but they do know that Profumo is aware of the position and that such action as is possible is being taken by his solicitors with the newspaper. They believe it to be true that Profumo has told the Prime Minister of the matter but they do not know that for certain.
>
> I think it wise for us to stay out of this business and [the Security Service] agree.

The upshot of it all is that the Marylebone officers were aware of the security and political importance of Christine Keeler's and Stephen Ward's statements, and reported them to Special Branch. No possible criticism can be made of the Marylebone officers. But the Criminal Investigation Department and Special Branch did, I think, make an error in not following up these reports by seeing Christine Keeler, or making sure she was seen, or by seeing Stephen Ward. This error was due to an error in coordination, for which no one individual can be blamed. But allowing for this error, the gist of the information was passed on by Special Branch to the Security Service. And thenceforward the responsibility for further action rested with the Security Service. I will deal with this when I consider the operation of the Security Service.

It may be asked why did not the police themselves report these matters to the Home Secretary. The answer is, I think, this: In so far as it involved a security matter they fulfilled their duty by reporting it to the Special Branch. In so far as it involved private morals it would not be for them to report it to anyone. It would be contrary to our way of thinking that police should be expected to report to the Home Secretary, or indeed to the Prime Minister, anything they happen incidentally to discover affecting the moral character or behaviour of any individual, including even a Minister of the Crown.

The lawyers are called in

No one can understand what happened at this time unless he realizes the extreme anxiety felt by Stephen Ward, Mr Profumo and, I may add, Lord Astor, over the critical 10 days, Monday, 28th January 1963 to Wednesday, 6th February 1963. They were very anxious that nothing should be disclosed prejudicial to their good names. Each instructed lawyers to protect his interests. And, as it happened, the main burden was borne by Stephen Ward's Counsel (Stephen Ward's Counsel was Mr Rees-Davies, MP in all the stages in this chapter) and by Mr Profumo's solicitors (Theodore Goddard & Co.). By Friday, 1st February 1963 they had discovered these disturbing facts:

- They got to know Christine Keeler had signed a conditional contract to sell her story to the *Sunday Pictorial* for £1,000, of which £200 was paid down, but they did not know what her story contained. In particular they did not know what she had told the newspaper about Stephen Ward, Mr Profumo or Lord Astor. They got to know that arrangements had been made for her to sign the proofs of her story early in the week beginning Monday, 4th February, and also for her to be accommodated at the expense of the newspaper in a flat at The White House, Albany Street. Once the proofs were signed by her as correct, the newspaper would be free to publish the article without fear of any libel action by her, though they would, of course, be liable to libel actions if they made defamatory statements which were untrue about anyone else.
- They got to know that the case of John Edgecombe was in the list for trial at the Session at the Central Criminal Court starting on Tuesday, 5th February, and Christine Keeler might have to attend any day. The

case was expected to be tried that week, and should be finished by the Friday. Christine Keeler was to be an important witness and might be subjected to cross-examination as to her credit and as to her character, and she might bring out their names. Until the trial was over the newspaper might not feel able to print her story, because the matter might be prejudicial to the trial and a contempt of court. Once the case was over, the newspaper would be able to publish the articles without fear of being in contempt of court.

It was important therefore to do everything possible in law to stop the newspaper publishing the story of Christine Keeler. Here the lawyers were in a difficulty. In the ordinary way it is very difficult to get an injunction to stop the publication of defamatory matter: if the defendants swear that the words are true and that they intend to justify them, the court will rarely intervene to stop them; the court will not prejudge the question whether the words are true or not. But in this case there appeared a way to overcome that rule of law. Christine Keeler had told her story to several people, including newspaper reporters, and it had been repeated by others. It was suggested that a writ for slander be issued against her and others in respect of these statements. If such a writ were issued and the newspapers were notified of it, the matter would become *sub judice*. The newspapers would not, it was thought, publish her story because they would be in danger of being in contempt of court – in respect of the slander action. This plan required a good deal of work, such as taking statements from witnesses, preparing draft writs and so forth.

While preparing that plan, however, for legal proceedings, an alternative proposal was made, namely to see Christine Keeler, to see how far she had gone with the newspaper and see if she could be persuaded not to publish her story. There were long conferences between Stephen Ward's counsel and Mr Profumo's solicitor on Saturday and Sunday, 2nd and 3rd February 1963. Both felt that, if negotiations of this kind were to be pursued, it was very desirable that Christine Keeler, for her own protection, should be advised by a solicitor. It was essential that she should not be advised by the solicitor to the newspaper, but be separately advised by her own solicitor. In a day or two Christine Keeler did go to a solicitor. It appears that on Saturday afternoon, 2nd February 1963 Mr Profumo's solicitors went to see her and, after some discussion about the contract, gave her the name of a solicitor and also their own telephone number. The impression they got was that she wanted money. She did not go to the solicitor that they suggested. Then Stephen Ward's counsel suggested the name of another solicitor. He was a young man who was a former pupil of his at the bar and had since become a solicitor (Mr Gerald Black of Gerald Black & Co.). On Sunday, 3rd February 1963 Stephen Ward's counsel asked this young solicitor to come and see him and told him the outline of the story. There was an intervening approach through a friend and on 4th February 1963 at 4.30 p.m. Christine Keeler went to see this solicitor. She was accompanied, not by this friend, but by Paul Mann.

It is quite clear that the negotiations had these objectives: on the one hand Christine Keeler was to withdraw from her contract with the newspaper, so that her story would not be published, and she was to go away for a while immediately after the Edgecombe trial; on the other hand she was to be paid compensation in money for the loss of her contract and for the expenses to which she would be put.

The negotiations are of importance because in the debate on 17th June 1963 it was suggested by Sir Lionel Heald, QC, MP, in the House of Commons that on 4th February 1963 there was an approach which appeared to indicate a demand for money.

Now I desire to say, in fairness to all concerned, that there was nothing unlawful in these negotiations, provided always that Christine Keeler had not the intention to extort money but only to receive a fair recompense. The law on the matter is laid down in Section 31 (2) of the Larceny Act 1916, which says that 'every person who, *with intent to extort any valuable thing from any person* directly or indirectly proposes to abstain from, or offers to prevent, the publishing of *any matter or thing* touching any other person, shall be guilty of a misdemeanour'. I have italicized the important words for present purposes. The words 'any matter or thing' show that, whatever the matter about to be published, that is to say whether it be libel or no libel (see Regina v. Coghlan (1865) 4 Foster and Finlayson 316 at page 321 by Bramwell B), true or untrue (see Rex v. Wyatt (1921) 16 Criminal Appeal Reports 57), nevertheless it is an offence to propose to abstain from the publishing of it if it is done with intent to extort money. There need not be an express request for money. It can be implied. Even to say 'If you make it worth my while, nothing will appear in the Press' will suffice, provided always there is an intention to extort money (see Regina v. Menage 3 Foster and Finlayson 310). Truth is no answer to the charge. The greater the truth, the greater the weapon in the hand of the blackmailer. The gist of the offence is the intention to extort. Such is the law if done by one alone. If the attempt to extort is done by two or more in combination – by threatening exposure even of the truth – it is indictable as a conspiracy at common law (see Rex v. Hollingberry (1825) 4 Barnewell and Cresswell 329).

Now for the negotiations themselves. There is some controversy as to what took place which I feel I cannot resolve. So I set down the versions on either side of the critical conversations. The name of Paul Mann comes again into the story at this point. During these critical days of early February 1963 Stephen Ward and Christine Keeler had quarrelled, but Paul Mann still remained friendly with both and acted as intermediary between them. On Saturday evening, 2nd February 1963, Stephen Ward took Paul Mann to see Stephen Ward's counsel in his private house and counsel saw him alone. According to counsel's note made shortly afterwards Paul Mann said:

> I think that Christine should be made to deny everything and talk proposition-wise as to what it is worth for her to be quiet. I think she is open to a higher bid. She is not satisfied with £1,000. I told her she ought to have obtained a good deal more.

According to Paul Mann himself, he said,

> I was myself quite concerned with people's reputations and one thing and another and the possible scandal that the papers could make of the whole thing. I said I did not know what she was going to do, but I said I would be only too willing to take her away after the trial and to keep the Press away from her. I remember saying, too, that I certainly could not do it all on my own funds, but I was quite prepared to make it a holiday for myself. There were no sums mentioned.

Both agreed that counsel broke off the conversation and said he could not discuss the proposition, and told Paul Mann that he should get Christine Keeler to go and see a solicitor.

On Monday afternoon, 4th February 1963, at about 4.30 p.m., Paul Mann accompanied Christine Keeler to the solicitor whose name had been mentioned by Stephen Ward's counsel. She went in to see the solicitor whilst Paul Mann sat outside next to the switchboard. She brought with her the telephone number of Mr Profumo's solicitor, and after taking her instructions the solicitor telephoned Mr Profumo's solicitor. There is a controversy as to the opening words: Christine Keeler's solicitor says that he said to Mr Profumo's solicitor, 'I understand your clients have offered to help her financially', and he said 'Yes'. Whereas Mr Profumo's solicitor denies that any such opening took place. Save for that controversy it seems clear that the substance of the conversation was as follows:

Christine Keeler's solicitor told Mr Profumo's solicitor that he was acting for Christine, that she did not wish to harm Mr Profumo in any way, but she had no one to turn to for financial assistance except the newspaper. She was due to see the newspaper later that afternoon and the newspaper had arranged for her to stay at the White House. If she did not continue to help the newspaper with the publication she would be without money. Christine Keeler's solicitor said he thought that the criminal proceedings against John Edgecombe would probably be on that week and that she intended to go away after the trial. She proposed to go abroad, to America. She was to receive from the newspaper £1,500 for six articles or £1,000 for four. Christine Keeler's solicitor said they did not want to publish and that the matter was a delicate one. One of them asked the other what he had in mind (there is some controversy on this) and after a little to and fro Christine Keeler's solicitor said £3,000. Mr Profumo's solicitor said he would take instructions. A very short time later, however, Christine Keeler's solicitor (who had Christine present with him) telephoned to Mr Profumo's solicitor and said that she would need £5,000 as she wanted to get a house for her parents. Mr Profumo's solicitor said he would have to put the matter to his client. Christine's solicitor said he would await an answer. None came; so he himself telephoned, but was told Mr Profumo's solicitor had gone out.

Meanwhile what had happened was this: Mr Profumo's solicitors regarded the request for £5,000 as so serious that they went round that evening to seek the advice of Queen's Counsel (Mr Mark Littman, QC) and then, with him and Mr Profumo, they went to see the Attorney-General, Sir John Hobson, and told him of it. The Attorney-General thought it should be referred to the Director of Public Prosecutions. Mr Profumo said that he was prepared to prosecute if the Director thought it desirable. The next morning Mr Profumo's legal advisers explained the matter to the Director of Public Prosecutions who advised against a prosecution.

In view of what I have said earlier on the law, the question whether there was an offence or no in asking for money depended on whether there was an intent to extort or not. If it was a fair recompense, there would be nothing unlawful. Upon this point Christine Keeler's solicitor explained to me that, in mentioning £3,000, he was thinking of what it would cost to have her represented by counsel, what it would cost to have her protected at the trial by an ex-CID officer or something like that, what it would cost to put her parents in a house somewhere, and that she wanted to go off to America after the trial of John Edgecombe for a holiday. After he put the telephone down Christine Keeler said, 'I think you ought to have asked for £5,000. How much is the house going to cost?' The solicitor said, '£2,000 up to £3,000'. She said: 'It will cost me £500 whilst I am away in America. I would like to have something to come back to. I would like you to phone and say £5,000.' So he did so.

I would like to say, in fairness to Christine Keeler's solicitor, that he had only been brought into the case at very short notice and had no time to reflect. It was a situation entirely out of the ordinary. He told me he thought the £5,000 was nothing to the persons concerned and it did seem a pretty fair estimate of what Christine Keeler would be involved in. Having seen him, I am sure he had no intention to extort and ought fairly to be excused for what does look, I confess, at first sight a most unjustifiable suggestion.

As for Christine Keeler, it is only fair to say that, if she had been minded to blackmail Mr Profumo, she would probably have kept the 'Darling' letter herself and not handed it over to the *Sunday Pictorial*. Further, I would record her statement to me: When £3,000 was mentioned, she says, 'I said No, and I know this sounds wicked, I said £5,000 because I wanted to move my parents, you see, so I do admit that I did say to raise it … It was not a matter of blackmail. I would have asked for £50,000 if it was.' Let no one judge her too harshly. She was not yet 21. And since the age of 16 she had become enmeshed in a net of wickedness. I would credit her, too, with a desire only for a fair recompense and not an intention to extort.

It is quite clear that after the telephone conversation on 4th February 1963 Mr Profumo's solicitors had no negotiations with Christine Keeler or anyone on her behalf to pay her any money. But Stephen Ward's counsel had negotiations with Christine's solicitors to which I must now turn.

On the next day, 5th February 1963, Christine Keeler's solicitor was speaking, he told me, to Ward's counsel on another matter, and afterwards they got on to the subject of Christine. Christine's solicitor said he was acting for her and said, 'She says she would like to have five' (meaning £5,000). Stephen Ward's counsel (presumably acting on behalf of Stephen Ward) said, 'Oh, I am sure that will be all right, I will let you know.' Christine's solicitor said it was most urgent. That afternoon Christine's solicitor went and collected £50 in cash from Stephen Ward's counsel. Christine's solicitor gave her £20 of the £50 and she agreed not to go to the White House (the flat provided by the newspaper). Next day Christine's solicitor went to collect the balance of the £5,000, as he thought. Stephen Ward's counsel gave him a packet which he opened. Inside was £450. It then became clear, he told me, that when he had said 'five' on the telephone, Stephen Ward's counsel had thought he meant £500, not £5,000. Christine's solicitor said he could not take the £450. He went back and told her what had happened. She thought she had been tricked. She would not dream of accepting the money. She would print. That is the last the solicitor saw of her.

Stephen Ward's counsel gave me an account which corresponded in most of the essentials. He told me that when Christine's solicitor said she wanted 'five in expenses', he took it to mean £500, not £5,000. This accorded exactly with what the expenses were to his mind. He worked them out in this way: As she had already received £200 from the newspaper, she ought to repay it to them. That made £200. Then she ought to be accommodated in a hotel over the trial which would cost £100. And she ought to have £200 to be away after the trial for the next fortnight. Stephen Ward's counsel told me that Christine's solicitor said it was most urgent and, on that account, he did let him have £50 in cash out of his own pocket that afternoon. On the next day he reported it to his solicitor who also thought £500 was a proper sum. So he made arrangements with Stephen Ward and got the money from him. He offered the £450 to Christine's solicitor, but he did not accept it.

Stephen Ward got the £500 in this way. He asked Lord Astor to lend it to him: and Lord Astor (after consulting his solicitor) did so. But Stephen Ward did not disclose to Lord Astor the precise purpose of the £500. The knowledge which Lord Astor had is shown by two letters of 6th February which record the transaction. Stephen Ward wrote on 6th February:

Dear Bill,
As I told you I have become involved in legal proceedings which are likely to involve me in heavy expenses and if you could lend me £500 I should be very grateful indeed.
Yours ever,
Stephen

Lord Astor replied on the same day, 6th February:

> So sorry to hear of your difficulty – I will be very glad to lend you
> £500. Pay me back when you can, or you can work some of it off
> in treatment, should I have any sprains, bruises or hunting
> accidents.

At the same time Lord Astor drew a cheque for £500 in Stephen
Ward's favour dated 6th February 1963. Stephen Ward had no
banking account so he could not pay it into his own account. But
the cheque, or the cash it represented, came into the hands of his
counsel. He repaid himself the £50 and offered the £450 to
Christine's solicitor.

After £450 was refused Stephen Ward's solicitor collected the
£450 from counsel that afternoon and placed it to the credit of
Stephen Ward on their client's account. There it remained until it
was withdrawn by Stephen Ward – £150 on 20th February 1963
and the balance on 15th March 1963. Stephen Ward used the
money to pay his rent and other personal debts. None of it went
to Christine Keeler or anyone on her behalf.

Pending the negotiations about £5,000, Christine Keeler had
not gone to sign the proofs of her article for the newspaper. She
had made excuses and kept away. But when the negotiations broke
down she went back to the newspaper. She went and signed the
proofs on 8th February 1963.

Ministers are concerned

The Ministers were concerned from a very early stage. Mr Profumo saw the Attorney-General on 28th January 1963, before he saw any lawyer of his own. And a week later, on 4th February 1963, he saw the Chief Whip. These Ministers played a very important part in what took place.

No one can understand the part played by the Law Officers in the Profumo affair unless it is realized that, by a convention which is well accepted, any of the Ministers of the Crown (who thinks he may be involved in litigation) is entitled to consult the Law Officers and ask their advice. In particular, when a Minister feels that his good name is being assailed, he is entitled to consult the Law Officers and ask them whether anything said about him is actionable as a libel or slander, and if it is, whether it is convenient from the point of view of the Government that he should bring an action.

It must also be remembered that at the end of January or in early February 1963 the Law Officers were closely concerned with Lord Radcliffe's enquiry into the Vassall case[*]. They had given advice to the Ministers whose names were mentioned there. They had very much in mind the position of Mr Galbraith. Here was a Minister against whom allegations had been made and who had resigned his office. Rumours had spread about him in the Press and in the House of Commons. Yet the evidence against him had, in the course of the inquiry, been shown to be utterly false, and the charge had been disproved. The inquiry had not been con-

[*] The 1963 Vassall (or Radcliffe) Tribunal, chaired by Lord Radcliffe, followed the jailing for 18 years of the Admiralty clerk John Vassall, a homosexual who had been blackmailed into spying for the KGB.

Viscount Astor with his bride, the fashion model Bronwen Pugh, after their wedding at Hampstead Registry Office, 1960

cluded – it was not concluded until 5th April 1963 – but the Law Officers had already heard enough to be able to form a good opinion as to the outcome.

Such is the background. On 28th January 1963 Stephen Ward's counsel asked to see the Attorney-General. The Attorney-General was engaged at the Vassall case, so the Solicitor-General saw him instead. Stephen Ward's counsel told the Solicitor-General that a young girl proposed to write a story for a newspaper telling of her relationship with various people, amongst whom was Lord Astor and Mr Profumo. The Solicitor-General felt that, as Mr Profumo's name was mentioned, the Law Officers were interested. And when the Attorney-General got back from the Vassall case at 4.30 p.m, the Solicitor-General said to him: 'Here is another of these rumours concerning another Minister, Mr Profumo.' As a Minister was involved the Attorney-General thought it was his duty to see whether he was going to bring a libel action and, if so, to say he was available to help. So the Attorney-General wrote him a note asking him to come and see him. And that night at about 11 p.m. Mr Profumo went to see the Attorney-General at his own home.

As this first interview is of considerable importance I must deal with it in some detail. The Attorney-General began by telling Mr Profumo that he must be absolutely frank with him, and that unless he was going to tell the truth, he was not prepared to help him. Mr Profumo told the Attorney-General that he had first met Christine Keeler at Cliveden when his wife and many other people were present; that shortly after he had gone to Stephen Ward's flat for a drink at his invitation and that thereafter he had done so on several occasions when Christine Keeler was among the guests. Mr Profumo said that twice when he arrived Christine Keeler was there alone and there had been a period when they were alone together before other people arrived. Mr Profumo asserted the complete innocence of his friendship with her and said that not only had there been no adultery but no sexual impropriety of any kind whatsoever. Mr Profumo said that he recollected having written to her one short note which he thought began with the word 'darling' telling her that he could not come to a cocktail party. He wrote this note, he said, on the day when he had been seen by the security people and warned by them not to go to Stephen Ward's flat because one of Ward's friends was a member of the Russian Embassy. Mr Profumo said that this was the total limit of his acquaintance with this girl. He had now heard that, based on this association and the one letter, Christine Keeler (who had recently become a drug addict, had been sleeping with West Indians and was short of money) was proposing to sell a false story to the newspapers which would ruin him.

The Attorney-General questioned Mr Profumo about everything which he told him and emphasized again the vital importance of his telling him the complete truth. He told him that if there was any truth in these rumours, he would have to resign. Mr Profumo reiterated the complete innocence of his friendship with Christine Keeler and explained that he commonly used the word 'darling' but said this was of no consequence as, being married to an actress, he had got into the habit of using this term of endearment which was quite meaningless.

The Attorney-General told Mr Profumo that if his story was true, he would have to take proceedings as soon as he had proof of any publication of any such story. Mr Profumo again repeated that there was nothing in these rumours. The Attorney-General then advised him to instruct the best possible solicitors and, that day or next morning, suggested that he should get in touch with Mr Derek Clogg, a senior partner in Theodore Goddard & Co., a solicitor of high repute and wide experience.

After hearing Mr Profumo's story the Attorney-General was

suspicious. He thought it was rather odd. And he retained a reasonable incredulity about it. He reported the matter to the Chief Whip and discussed the matter with the Solicitor-General.

A few days later the Attorney-General went to Mr Profumo's room, and he asked the Solicitor-General to come too. The Solicitor-General emphasized to Mr Profumo how vital it was, in his own interests and those of everyone, that he should be absolutely frank. Mr Profumo said he understood that, and he repeated more shortly and in broad outline what he had told the Attorney-General on 28th January, adding that at one of the cocktail parties he had given Christine Keeler a lighter which was not at all valuable but which she had admired when he used it. The Solicitor-General asked Mr Profumo whether in those circumstances he was prepared to issue a writ for slander or libel if he was advised that a proper opportunity presented itself. Mr Profumo said that he most certainly would, even if it were against a friend or colleague. The Solicitor-General reminded him of the effect of such a course of action if there was any chance that any defendant could prove that Mr Profumo had been guilty of adultery. Mr Profumo replied that he was aware of that, but that not every man who was alone with a woman and called her 'darling' committed adultery with her. Whatever might be said, he was not guilty of any improper conduct with Christine Keeler or of anything except the friendship of which he had told the Attorney-General. Mr Profumo said that he appreciated that of course it now all looked different, particularly because of the deterioration in manner and recent conduct of the girl, but that at the time when he knew her she was very different.

Mr Profumo said that he knew that (because of those few meetings and because he had been alone with her only for a short time and before others had arrived) he now faced ruin for himself and his family. He knew, he said, that in the particular climate of opinion then prevailing (the Radcliffe Tribunal was still sitting) there would be those who would disbelieve him, but that it would be grossly unfair that he should be driven from public life and into ruin when he was totally innocent and that he should become a victim of malevolent gossip, some of which was seeking to do to him what it had tried to do shortly before to one of his colleagues. Mr Profumo insisted again, with vehemence, that he had not committed adultery and that, although he would naturally prefer that the gossip should die down, if anything was ever published or if he could identify a gossipmonger, he would sue, no matter who it was.

On Sunday evening, 3rd February, Mr Profumo came with his solicitor (Mr Clogg) to see the Attorney-General at his home. There was a general discussion in which Mr Clogg made it clear that Mr Profumo had told him just the same as he had previously told the Attorney-General; in particular that Mr Profumo's relationship with Christine Keeler was entirely innocent.

On Monday evening, 4th February, the Attorney-General again saw Mr Profumo. Mr Profumo had with him his leading counsel and his solicitor. They reported to the Attorney-General the request for £5,000 made by Christine Keeler, through her solicitor, to Mr Profumo. The Attorney-General thought it was serious and advised Mr Profumo that the facts should be placed before the Director of Public Prosecutions. The Attorney-General took the view that there would only be an offence if the proposed publication was untrue and libellous. (Note: I do not myself share this view. Even if true, it would, I think, be an offence, if done with intent to extort.) And he was impressed by the fact that Mr Profumo was ready to prosecute. If a prosecution was brought, Mr Profumo would have to give evidence on oath about his relationship with Christine Keeler.

Up till this time the Attorney-General had been dubious whether Mr Profumo was telling the truth. He was keeping the matter in suspense. But when he found that Mr Profumo was prepared to bring an action for libel, and had actually instructed his solicitor to do so, and that he was prepared to prosecute on the request for £5,000, he did not see how he could disbelieve Mr Profumo and decided there was no reason why he should not accept his story. We now know that on Tuesday, 5th February 1963 Mr Profumo and his solicitor did see the Director of Public Prosecutions, who advised against a prosecution. But that does not affect the argument. What impressed the Attorney-General was the readiness of Mr Profumo to prosecute.

No one can understand the role of the Chief Whip (Mr Martin Redmayne, MP) in this matter unless he realizes that he is very concerned with the good name of the Government and the Ministers who comprise it. If rumours are about which may embarrass the Government, it is the business of the Chief Whip to know of them and to report them to the Prime Minister. The Chief Whip was very concerned at this time with the rumours about Mr Galbraith (which were subsequently shown in Lord Radcliffe's inquiry to be completely unfounded). So he was concerned here with the rumours about Mr Profumo.

In order to see how the Chief Whip came into the matter, I must first refer to a very important thing which happened. On the afternoon of Friday, 1st February 1963 a senior executive of a newspaper telephoned Admiralty House and asked to see the Prime Minister. As the Prime Minister was away in Italy and would not be back until the evening of Sunday, 3rd February, the executive called at Admiralty House and gave this information to one of his Secretaries, who recorded it in this note:

The object of his call concerned a security matter. … Mr Profumo had compromised himself with a girl who was involved with a negro in a case about attempted murder. … This girl's story has been sold to the Daily Mirror Group and it will include passages in which she was involved with Mr Profumo and in which the Russian Naval Attaché also figured. … Mr Profumo is alleged to have met this girl 'Kolania' through Lord Astor at Cliveden, where they chased her naked round the bathing pool. … It is also alleged that (i) 'Kolania' got into this company through the agency of a Mr Ward, who was a 'psychopathic specialist' of Wimpole Street; (ii) Mr Profumo, visiting 'Kolania' in Mr Ward's house, passed in the passage the Russian Naval Attaché on his way out from 'Kolania'; (iii) 'Kolania' has two letters on War Office paper signed 'J' – although it is not suggested that these letters are anything more than ones of assignation.

On receipt of this minute the Prime Minister's Principal Private Secretary asked the Deputy Director-General of the Security Service to come to Admiralty House. His object was simply to tell him about it and to get any information which might be helpful for him (the Private Secretary) to report to the Prime Minister. The Private Secretary handed the Deputy Director-General the note and asked if he had any comments. The Deputy Director-General said that very recently the Director-General had had a confidential talk with Mr Profumo in which Mr Profumo had recounted a story that was recognizably the same story. But that the girl was called Christine and not Kolania; that Mr Ward was Stephen Ward, and that he was not a 'psychopathic specialist' but an osteopath.

The Deputy Director-General told the Private Secretary that these confidences seemed to have been made by Mr Profumo in the hope that there might be security grounds for taking action with the Press, by D-notice or otherwise, to prevent publication. But this hope was a vain one. The Deputy Director-General and the Private Secretary agreed that the first step was to tell Mr

Profumo what had been said and ask if there was any truth in it. The Private Secretary said he would try and do it that evening. Mr Profumo would then have to decide whether he should tender his resignation to the Prime Minister or not. The Private Secretary said it would be necessary for him to give the information to the Chief Whip and also to tell the Prime Minister on his return from Italy.

Late that evening the Private Secretary called on Mr Profumo and explained that they had had a story about an article that might possibly appear in the Press and which would show him in a bad light. He told him that normally he would have reported it to the Prime Minister, but he was out of the country. Mr Profumo said that he had been in continuous touch during that week with the Attorney-General and the Solicitor-General and he was also being advised by a private firm of solicitors. His solicitor had spoken to someone who was going to put pressure on the *Sunday Pictorial* not to publish these articles. His solicitor was also seeing the girl in question at her request since she said she was in trouble. Mr Profumo suggested that the Private Secretary need not bother the Prime Minister at this stage. But the Private Secretary said it seemed of great importance that Mr Profumo should see the Chief Whip without delay. Mr Profumo said he would do so.

It should be mentioned here that on Sunday, 3rd February 1963 the *News of the World* published a picture of Christine Keeler saying that she was to be a witness in the shooting case I have described earlier. Most people seeing that picture would realize what she was.

Mr Profumo saw the Chief Whip on Monday, 4th February, at 12 noon. The Prime Minister's Private Secretary was present. Mr Profumo outlined the story for the benefit of the Chief Whip. The events referred to had all taken place between July and December of 1961. He had been at the bathing pool in July when there had been a pretty cheerful party but everybody had bathing costumes on. Mr Profumo said he had subsequently, in order to get a giggle in the evening, gone round to Stephen Ward's flat to meet a few young people and have a drink before dinner. Mr Profumo said that most of the young ladies to be found at this flat were not the sort of people one would wish to accompany one to a constituency meeting. But his wife had many theatrical friends and he was used to relaxing in this *galère*. Mr Profumo said that there had been a letter which started 'My Darling' but it had been quite harmless. He also admitted to a small present – a cigarette lighter. His lawyers had arranged to meet Christine Keeler on Saturday, 2nd February. She had said that the money the newspapers were offering her for her story was not enough and she wanted more. She refused to say that any of the stories that had been put about were untrue. She made it clear that money was what she wanted. Mr Profumo said he had been told by Sir Norman Brook (who had been advised by MI5) to see as little as possible of Stephen Ward since there was a security problem involved. Mr Profumo said that his lawyers had advised him to do nothing but to wait and see what, if anything, the newspaper published. If this was libellous he could then issue a writ. The Attorney-General and the Solicitor-General were advising him in the same sense. Mr Profumo added that he had made a full report on the position to the Head of the Security Service.

Mr Profumo asked if he should tell the Prime Minister at this stage. The Chief Whip thought that it was not necessary. Mr Profumo and the Chief Whip discussed the current rumours and Mr Profumo asked whether the Chief Whip thought he should resign on account of them. The Chief Whip said that, if they were true, of course he should resign, but if untrue it would be a great mistake. The thing was to wait for the newspaper articles if they appeared – which, he understood, might be in a fortnight – and then the position would have to be looked at again. Mr Profumo said that he had never met the Russian Assistant Naval Attaché at Stephen Ward's flat. He had been present at the bathing party in the summer. The only other time he had met him was when, accompanied by his wife, he went to the Gagarin Reception – and had reason to remember Mr Ivanov as he promised to get them a vodka and went off, never to be seen again.

Such was the story told by Mr Profumo to the Chief Whip and from which he never resiled. When the Chief Whip, to test him took the line, 'Well, look, nobody would believe that you didn't sleep with her', Mr Profumo made the disarming answer, 'Yes, I know they wouldn't believe it, but it happens to be true that I didn't sleep with her'. He assured the Chief Whip repeatedly that what he said was true and that he was waiting for an opportunity to take action to refute the story. The Chief Whip was kept informed by the Attorney-General of the various discussions which he had had with Mr Profumo. Just as the Attorney-General felt that they must accept his version as true, so did the Chief Whip. The Attorney-General explained to the Chief Whip from time to time that, if any publication was made, a writ would be issued, but that no opportunity had yet occurred.

The first opportunity to bring an action came when a private newsletter called the *Westminster Confidential* gave mention to the rumours. This is a typewritten letter, stencilled and distributed to 200 or so subscribers. In an issue dated 8th March 1963 this newsletter referred to the fact that the girls had started selling their stories to the Sunday newspapers and added:

One of the choicest bits in their stories was a letter, apparently signed 'Jock', on the stationery of the Secretary for War. The allegation by this girl was that not only was this Minister, who has a famous actress as his wife, her client, but also the Soviet Military

Christine Keeler at home, June 1963

Attaché, apparently a Colonel Ivanov. The famous actress wife, of course, would sue for divorce, the scandal ran. Who was using the call-girl to 'milk' whom of information – the War Secretary or the Soviet Military Attaché? – ran the minds of those primarily interested in security..

This newsletter did not come at once to the knowledge of Mr Profumo or the Chief Whip or the Attorney-General. They got to know if it about 13th March.

The question has been asked why an action for libel was not taken on this publication. It was clearly defamatory of Mr Profumo. If he was seeking an opportunity to vindicate himself, why not bring an action? The answer is that it was considered by Mr Profumo and his legal adviser and also the Attorney-General. Mr Profumo's legal adviser was disinclined to take action. He did not think this was the right occasion to sue. The Attorney-General agreed with this view. The *Westminster Confidential* had too small a circulation, and contained scandal about someone else, too, which ought not to be made public. It was very probable that this publication of the *Westminster Confidential* was only the beginning, so that very soon stories might begin to appear in the national Press. It was better, therefore, to wait for a more substantial publication.

The opportunity to refute the rumours was not long in coming. It came in a fortnight. But it came in an unexpected form. On 21st March 1963 Members of Parliament made statements in the House of Commons. Meanwhile many things had happened. Christine Keeler had disappeared. She did not appear to give evidence at the Edgecombe trial. And to add to all the previous rumours, there was a new one – that Mr Profumo had helped her to disappear.

The disappearance of Christine Keeler

One of the matters that has given rise to much public uneasiness is Christine Keeler's disappearance in March 1963, with the result that she never appeared to give evidence at the trial of John Edgecombe. She was taken to Spain by Paul Mann. It is suggested that this was procured by people in high places because they were afraid their names might come out in her evidence at the trial. If this be the case, then it would be, of course, a very serious matter.

The law is this: If a witness, who is bound over by recognizance to appear to give evidence does not come forward at the trial, his liability depends whether there is good excuse or not. If he or she has a good excuse – as, for instance, is ill and cannot come – it is no breach of recognizance. But if he or she has no good excuse, then the recognizance is liable to be forfeited. In this case Christine Keeler was bound over in the sum of £40 and she forfeited that sum. But there is this further law: It is a criminal offence for two or more persons to conspire together to obstruct the course of justice by getting a witness to disappear (see Rex v. Steventon (1802) 2 East 362). And in seeing whether persons have been guilty of a conspiracy, it was said by Lord Campbell when Lord Chief Justice of England: 'If the necessary effect of the agreement was to defeat the ends of justice, that must be taken to be the object' (see Regina v. Hamp and others (1852) 6 Cox Criminal Cases at p. 172). [I think must should probably be read as may.]

Such being the law I have looked to see whether there is any evidence of any such conspiracy.

Before considering Christine Keeler's disappearance in March, I must refer to what happened early in February 1963 when the John Edgecombe case was expected to come on shortly. Stephen

Ward's solicitor told me that he was scared that Christine Keeler would disappear: 'The one thing I was afraid of was that Christine Keeler, a material witness in the Edgecombe trial, would be spirited out of the country.' I asked him, 'Why did you fear that?' His answer was: 'Simply because of various things Ward said to me.' The solicitor gave Stephen Ward this firm and wise advice, 'On no account must any of us be a party to that thing.'

About that very time, early in February 1963, Paul Mann (on his own admission to me) made this suggestion to Stephen Ward's counsel (I have already quoted it, but it is so important that at this point I repeat it):

> I said I did not know what she was going to do, but I said I would be only too willing to take her away after the trial and to keep the Press away from her. I remember saying, too, that I certainly could not do it all on my own funds but I was quite prepared to make a holiday for myself.

I asked Paul Mann the question: 'They wanted her to disappear after the trial?' He replied, 'No, this was purely a suggestion that she should disappear; nobody said, "Yes, we want her to go after the trial".'

I take it to be clear, therefore, that early in February 1963 Stephen Ward conceived the idea that Christine Keeler should disappear and mentioned it to Paul Mann; that Paul Mann was willing to assist in it; but that nothing was said expressly whether she was to disappear before or after the trial. It is equally clear that the lawyers would have nothing to do with it. It was on 5th February 1963 that Mr Profumo and his lawyer consulted the Director of Public Prosecutions. On 7th February Mr Profumo's solicitor told Stephen Ward's solicitor of the point. Stephen Ward's solicitor (who had on the day before approved the offer of

£500) told me: 'My amber light very quickly turned to red and I told my client on no account must he pay any money to her or her solicitor or to her account.' Even the £500 was not to be paid to her. He told me: 'The thing I was scared of from the very beginning was that Christine Keeler would be spirited away out of the country, and the last thing I wanted was for Stephen Ward to be concerned with that. And if she had disappeared abroad or had had £500 from us, it would have looked extremely fishy.'

As it happened the Edgecombe trial was postponed because of the illness of the mini-cab driver. It was adjourned until the next Sessions and was expected to come on for trial in March 1963. Meanwhile, however, from the first week in February 1963 Paul Mann was in close touch with Christine Keeler. He told me that he started to spend a tremendous amount of time with her; almost as it were keeping a 24-hour watch on her. The time came, he told me, when she was in a very distressed state and wanted to leave and get away from it all. She told me herself that she was in fear of two coloured men who had been paid to cut her up. She said: 'I knew it was my duty to go to the Court but to tell you the truth I thought, "To hell with my duty, I am not going to let people knock me about from here to there". I did not realize the seriousness of the consequences. I just decided to leave.' Paul Mann told me that he had himself been planning to have a holiday in Spain a little later but at Christine Keeler's request he brought his holiday forward about two weeks. The decision was taken about the end of February 1963 and they left on the night of Friday, 8th March 1963.

They went by car – Paul Mann, Christine Keeler and Kim Proctor. They told me they had very little money. Christine Keeler had £20 which she gave to Paul Mann. Kim Proctor put in money too. I asked Paul Mann what means he had at that time. He said: 'I had my own means, untraceable resources. It did really, leaving on Friday night, find us in a sticky position. Between the three of us, I

should think we had £100 and some dollars, but I had an insurance cheque for £175. The insurance company had an office in Spain, and I thought there would be no trouble in cashing it at all, but it turned out it took them practically four weeks to cash this cheque.' At any rate, with such means as they had, they drove across France and into Spain and disappeared. They went to a remote fishing village on the coast of Spain. No one discovered their whereabouts until they went to Madrid at the weekend 23rd/24th March 1963.

On Sunday, 24th March 1963 Paul Mann telephoned the British Embassy. Early on Monday, 25th March 1963 Christine Keeler appeared at a police station in Madrid and asked to stay the night. Newspaper reporters, she said, were besieging the flat where she was staying. The newspaper reporters did in fact find them. And they were quick to make a contract with her under which she would sell them the story of her disappearance. Paul Mann negotiated it. She was to get £2,000, of which 25 per cent (£500) went to Paul Mann. The newspaper reporters arranged accommodation for her, as she had nothing. They gave £45 to Paul Mann for immediate expenses. The rest was paid to them when they got back to England. On 28th March 1963 they brought Christine Keeler back to England and took her to Scotland Yard. On 1st April 1963 she went to the Central Criminal Court and her recognizance in the sum of £40 was forfeited for her non-appearance. Paul Mann did not return till some time later. He only came back on 12th June 1963.

If the intention of Paul Mann and Christine Keeler was to enable Christine Keeler to avoid being called as a witness in the Edgecombe trial, they succeeded completely. The trial of John Edgecombe was started on Thursday, 14th March 1963 and finished on Friday, 15th March 1963. Christine Keeler was of course missing. The prosecution could, no doubt, have applied for an adjournment if they had thought fit, and it would probably have

Christine Keeler on holiday in Spain, March 1963

been granted for she was an important witness. But the prosecution did not apply for an adjournment. Nor did the defence. So the case went on.

Rumours inevitably spread that an important witness had been got out of the way for political reasons. In view of these rumours I have made every endeavour to find out whether anyone paid money to Paul Mann to take Christine Keeler away. There has been much speculation that Mr Profumo or Lord Astor paid money to get her to disappear. I have looked closely into the matter.

Mr Profumo strongly denied that he had paid any money. He very frankly placed at my disposal all records of his bank accounts and of his dealings with shares. I have had these examined by an expert accountant who was nominated by me. He made a most exhaustive examination and made the most minute enquiries. All were answered to his complete satisfaction. I have been through his report myself and am satisfied that there is no trace whatever of any money being paid by Mr Profumo directly or indirectly to or for the benefit of Stephen Ward or Christine Keeler or Paul Mann or anyone who might conceivably have had a hand in her disappearance. All payments by Mr Profumo at all material times are fully accounted for. I hold the rumour to be entirely without foundation.

Lord Astor, too, strongly denied that he had paid any money. He himself was away in the United States at the time she disappeared. He was away from 27th February 1963 to 12th April 1963. He, too, very frankly placed all records of his bank accounts and financial dealings fully before me. I have had them examined by the same expert accountant nominated by me. He again made a most exhaustive examination and made more minute enquiries. All his queries have been satisfactorily answered. I have been through his report and there are only these payments by Lord Astor to or for Stephen Ward which I need mention:

- A cheque for £100 which is said to have been handed by Stephen Ward to the landlord of a flat in Comeragh Road. This was early in 1961 and had clearly no relevance to the disappearance of Christine Keeler.
- A cheque for £500 on 6th February 1963 which is dealt with earlier. As I have stated none of this was used to pay for the disappearance of Christine Keeler.
- A cheque for £200 on 8th May 1963. In April 1963 Stephen Ward had surrendered the tenancy of the cottage. Lord Astor paid this sum to Stephen Ward in respect of improvements made by him at the cottage. Stephen Ward used this to pay his solicitor's fees. None of it was used to pay for the disappearance of Christine Keeler.

There is no trace of any money being paid by Lord Astor to anyone in furtherance of the disappearance of Christine Keeler. All his payments have been fully and satisfactorily accounted for. I hold that in his case also the rumour is entirely without foundation.

Paul Mann strongly denied that he received any money. He has some resources but not from Mr Profumo or Lord Astor. When I asked about his bank account he did tell me: 'I have a couple of security boxes that nobody knows of. I keep everything very secretive. … the two security boxes are not in my name, entirely secret. I just don't like anybody knowing anything about me in that respect … but they certainly do not contain any such sums that were offered to me or given to me or supposed to be given to me. Whatever I have is entirely my own. It has not been gained by any weird ways.' I have no reason to doubt this statement.

I must add that there is no evidence whatever that Paul Mann or Christine Keeler received any money for her disappearance. It is quite clear that, on this trip to Spain, Paul Mann was very short of money. So was Christine Keeler. It must be remembered that she had lost her only contract with the newspapers. The *Sunday Pictorial* told her on 24th February 1963 that they were not going to publish her story. She had no further contract in the offing. The only pecuniary motive that has been suggested to me was this: It may be that they both foresaw that, if she disappeared, there would be a good story to sell to the newspapers and they hoped to find their reward that way. If so, they succeeded in their object.

I return therefore to my initial question: Is there any evidence of a conspiracy to obstruct the course of justice by causing Christine Keeler to disappear? There is no evidence whatever to implicate Mr Profumo or Lord Astor. There is, however, some evidence against Paul Mann and Christine Keeler: for the very fact of their concerted action in causing her to disappear is evidence sufficient for the purpose (see the dictum of Lord Campbell which I have already quoted). But it would be a question for a jury whether they did intend to obstruct the course of justice.

The Edgecombe trial

On 14th March 1963 John Edgecombe came up for trial at the Central Criminal Court before Mr Justice Thesiger and a jury. The indictments contained five counts: Count 1 dealt with the 'slashing'. It charged Edgecombe that on 27th October 1962 he wounded Gordon with intent to do him grievous bodily harm. Counts 2 to 5 dealt with the 'shooting'. They charged Edgecombe with these offences on 14th December 1962: shooting at Christine Keeler with intent to commit murder; shooting at her with intent to do grievous bodily harm; possessing a firearm with intent to endanger life; and having an offensive weapon without lawful authority.

Both counsel for the prosecution and for the defence knew that Christine Keeler, a very important witness, had disappeared, but neither applied for an adjournment and the trial proceeded without her evidence. Counsel for the prosecution simply said to the jury: 'I am unable to call the principal witness, Miss Keeler, before you. As far as the police are concerned, she has disappeared. It is nothing to do with the defendant.' The trial did not finish on 14th March 1963 but continued on to the 15th March 1963. In the result John Edgecombe was acquitted on the counts of shooting with intent to murder (Count 2) and shooting with intent to do grievous bodily harm (Count 3). He was also acquitted on the count of wounding Gordon on 27th October 1962 (Count 1). But he was convicted of possessing a firearm with intent to endanger life (Count 4). (The judge discharged the jury from giving a verdict on Count 5.)

After the verdict, evidence was given of John Edgecombe's character. In 1951 he was convicted of two cases of stealing, in

1959 for living on immoral earnings, and in 1962 for unlawful possession of dangerous drugs. The judge sentenced him to imprisonment for seven years. He appealed against his conviction and sentence, but on 27th May 1963 the Court of Criminal Appeal dismissed the appeal.

It seems plain that the absence of Christine Keeler had an important influence on the course of the case. As the Lord Chief Justice said, 'The fact that the jury acquitted on the first two [shooting] charges seems to this Court natural in the absence of the girl.' I may perhaps add that the acquittal on the 'slashing' charge seems natural also, in the absence of the girl over whom the men were quarrelling.

The Attorney-General, of course, had nothing to do with the prosecution of John Edgecombe. The first he heard of the disappearance of Christine Keeler was from the evening papers. Next day rumours were circulating round the Temple that an important witness had been got out of the way for political reasons and that some bargain had been made that the case should go on without her. I am satisfied that the lawyers for the prosecution were party to no such bargain. Counsel for the prosecution went to the Attorney-General and explained how it was that the case had proceeded without this witness. It was his decision alone and for these reasons: (a) He thought there was sufficient evidence without the missing witness; (b) John Edgecombe was in custody; and (c) the trial had already been postponed once because of the illness of a witness. I would not wish to question these reasons – they are cogent – but I think that, in the result, it was an unfortunate decision. It made it difficult for the prosecution to ask for a conviction of John Edgecombe on the charge of slashing 'Lucky' Gordon on 27th October 1962 and on the charges of shooting at Christine Keeler on 14th December 1962 with intent to murder her or cause her grievous bodily harm (John Edgecombe was not convicted on

Aloysius 'Lucky' Gordon and John Edgecombe, witnesses in the Profumo affair, being taken from Wandsworth jail for an interview with Lord Denning

any of these charges); and it made it possible for John Edgecombe to complain (as he complained to me) that he had no opportunity to cross-examine her as to her character and as to the fact that the gun was, as he said, her gun. (It is always a telling point for a defendant to say he had no opportunity to cross-examine the chief witness for the prosecution.) More important even than this, it heightened the suspicion that her disappearance was manoeuvred for political reasons. It was thought to be in Mr Profumo's interest that she should disappear and he was supposed to be at the back of it.

The Attorney-General made immediate inquiries into the matter. He saw Mr Profumo and asked him whether he had anything to do with the absence of Christine Keeler as a witness at the trial.

Press comment

It is time to revert to what the Press had been doing. It will be remembered that in early February 1963, when the Edgecombe case was expected any day, the *Sunday Pictorial* were thinking of publishing the story which Christine Keeler had given them. But Stephen Ward and his lawyers were doing all they could to stop publication. When the Edgecombe case was adjourned there was not the same urgency because nothing could be published till after the case. Nevertheless, Stephen Ward was not idle. He saw the newspaper, and also wrote to them, saying that Christine's story was untrue.

During the three days 19th to 21st February 1963 there were important discussions between the newspapermen, on the one hand, and Stephen Ward and his solicitor on the other hand. The upshot of this was a proposal that the newspaper should abandon Christine Keeler's story and publish Stephen Ward's story instead. This proposal was eventually found acceptable to all concerned. But there was no actual bargain about it. The newspaper realized that they could not safely publish Christine Keeler's story, but that they could safely publish Stephen Ward's. And that is what they decided to do. On Thursday, 28th February, the newspaper wrote to Christine Keeler saying that they had decided not to publish her story. This meant that she had to rest content with the £200 she had received – she lost all change of the balance of £800. About this time they made arrangements for Stephen Ward's story. They got it all ready for publication immediately after the Edgecombe trial.

The Edgecombe trial was held, as I have said, on 14th and 15th March 1963. On the very first day, Thursday, 14th March, the announcement was made that Christine Keeler was missing. This attracted much attention. On the very next day, Friday the 15th, whilst the case was still part heard, the *Daily Express* came out with the front-page banner headline 'War Minister Shock'. On the left-hand side there was a photograph of Mr and Mrs Profumo, with the comment:

> Mr John Profumo, the War Minister, has offered his resignation to Mr Macmillan for personal reasons. The Prime Minister is under-stood to have asked him to stay on. There has been speculation about Mr Profumo's future among MPs for several weeks. On the steps of his house in Chester Terrace, Regent's Park, he said: 'I have not seen the Prime Minister and I have not resigned – there is no reason why I should.' This is taken to mean that he has accept-ed the Prime Minister's request to stay.

On the right-hand side of the page there was a photograph of Christine Keeler headed 'Vanished Old Bailey Witness', and below:

> This is Christine Keeler, the 21-year-old model who was found to be missing yesterday when the Old Bailey trial of a man accused of attempting to murder her began. The jury was told: 'As far as the police are concerned, she has simply disappeared'.

On an inner page there were four striking photographs of Christine Keeler from which most people could readily infer her calling.

In point of fact, Mr Profumo had never seen the Prime Minister nor offered his resignation. All that had happened was that, six weeks earlier, he had seen the Chief Whip and asked if he ought to resign. He was told that if there was no truth in the rumours, he should not resign. The *Daily Express* was not the only newspaper to get the story of an offer of resignation. The *Liverpool Daily Post* had it also. The *Daily Express* told me that the juxtaposition of the two stories – Christine Keeler's disappearance and Mr Profumo's resignation – was entirely coincidental and supplemented this with reasons. Accepting this to be so, it had nevertheless unfortunate results. It is true, of course, that those of the readers who had not heard the rumours would not take it that there was any connection between the two stories. But it would seem that some of their readers, namely those who had heard the rumour of Mr Profumo's association with Christine Keeler, now added to it this further rumour that he was responsible for her disappearance. To them it would carry a defamatory meaning.

The front page of the *Daily Express* aroused a good deal of alarm. The Chief Whip felt the thing was getting out of hand. He asked whether it was actionable. On the self-same day, 15th March 1963, the Prime Minister himself discussed the position with the Attorney-General. The Attorney-General thought it would be premature to issue any writs or anything of that sort. He took the view that there was nothing in the newspaper that could be described as defamatory, and that the right course was to wait for the Sunday newspapers and see what, if anything, they published.

The *Sunday Pictorial* was waiting till after the Edgecombe case to publish Stephen Ward's story. It had been approved by Stephen Ward and his solicitors. The fee was to be £575, to be paid direct to Stephen Ward's solicitors. The reason was that Stephen Ward owed his solicitors about £475 for the costs of all they did to stop Christine Keeler's story, and his solicitors wanted to be sure of their money. As soon as the Edgecombe case was over, on Sunday, 17th March 1963, the *Sunday Pictorial* published Stephen Ward's story. They combined it with a cogent comment on the disappearance of Christine Keeler. On the front page there was a large photograph of her. Then below in large letters: 'The Model, MI5, the Russian Diplomat and Me, by Stephen Ward'. This was followed by:

> This is Christine Keeler, the 21-year-old red-head model whose name made news this week as the missing witness in an Old Bailey shooting trial. Christine knew a number of distinguished men in public life. Did she fear they might be named in the case? What is she like, this girl who came to London and became the friend of the famous and the wealthy? Who knows her better than Stephen Ward?

On the inside pages there was an article by Stephen Ward on 'My friendship with Christine'. But there was not a word about Mr Profumo in it, so it gave him no cause of action. A day or two later the newspaper paid Stephen Ward's solicitor £525 for the story, and that was the end of that transaction – subject, however, to the 'Darling' letter. But one important thing remained to be done. The *Sunday Pictorial* had all this time held in their safe the original of the 'Darling' letter, that is, the letter of 9th August 1961 by Mr Profumo to Christine Keeler. It was the most talked of unseen letter in London, but no one asked to see it. And they had photographs of it too. They had it in mind, of course. On 15th March 1963, when Stephen Ward's story had been accepted and the solicitor went to approve it, the newspaper editor mentioned the letter. He told Stephen Ward's solicitor: 'I have got in my possession the indiscreet letter. Once things are over and done with, I will let you have it.' This did not form part of the negotiations. There was no bargain about it.

The *Sunday Pictorial* continued to keep the letter. Even after the Edgecombe case no one asked to see it. Even after Mr Profumo's statement in the House on 22nd March 1963 no one asked to see it. But eventually the *Sunday Pictorial* did not want to keep it any more. They wanted to get rid of it and suggested to Stephen Ward's solicitor that he should have it. So on Wednesday, 3rd April 1963 Stephen Ward's solicitor went and got it from them. But both the newspaper and Stephen Ward's solicitor soon had second thoughts about the propriety of this. They seem to have come to the conclusion that the proper person to have the letter was Mr Profumo's solicitor, because the copyright in it belonged to Mr Profumo. So on 5th April Stephen Ward's solicitor handed it over to Mr Profumo's solicitor. But the newspaper kept their photographs of the letter. After all they had paid Christine Keeler £200. Maybe the photographs of the letter would come in useful one day.

The meeting of the five Ministers

The disappearance of Christine Keeler – and the front page of the *Daily Express* – had the inevitable result. Rumours multiplied that Mr Profumo was responsible for her disappearance. Within a week, on Thursday, 21st March 1963, these rumours found voice in the House of Commons. Shortly after 11 p.m. Mr George Wigg rose and said:

> There is not an Hon. Member in the House, nor a journalist in the Press Gallery, nor do I believe is there a person in the public gallery who, in the last few days, has not heard rumour upon rumour involving a Member of the Government Front Bench. ... I myself use the Privilege of the House of Commons – that is what it is giv-en me for – to ask the Home Secretary to go to the Despatch Box – he knows that the rumour to which I refer relates to Miss Christine Keeler and Miss Davies and a shooting by a West Indian – and on behalf of the Government, categorically deny the truth of these rumours ... on the other hand, if there is anything in them set up a Select Committee.

Mr Crossman supported him. About 11.50 p.m. Mrs Castle asked this question:

> What if it is a perversion of justice that is at stake? The Clerk of the Central Criminal Court is reported as saying: 'If any member of the public did know where Miss Keeler was, it is his or her duty to inform the police.' If accusations are made that there are people in high places who do know and are not informing the police, is it not a matter of public interest?

Christine Keeler in Cannes, France, May 1963

These were remarks of much significance. They clearly imputed that Mr Profumo had been responsible for the disappearance of Christine Keeler. There were four Ministers who were in the Chamber and heard these remarks, namely, Mr Henry Brooke, the Home Secretary, Mr William Deedes, the Minister without Portfolio, Sir John Hobson, the Attorney-General, and Sir Peter Rawlinson, the Solicitor-General. Mr Iain Macleod was in the Chamber for the last part and heard the whole of Mrs Castle's remarks. After the remarks were made, Mr William Deedes at once went out and reported them to the Chief Whip (Mr Martin Redmayne, who had not been in the Chamber). It was clear that Mr Henry Brooke would be expected to reply to them. He could not leave the Chamber, but the Chief Whip, with the assistance of the Attorney-General and the Solicitor-General, drafted out a form of words to suggest to him. Mr Brooke adopted them in his reply in these words:

> I do not propose to comment on rumours which have been raised under the cloak of Privilege and safe from any action at law. The Hon. Member for Dudley (Mr Wigg) and the Hon. Member for Blackburn (Mrs Castle) should seek other means of making these insinuations if they are prepared to substantiate them.

The debate ended at 1.22 a.m. and Mr Henry Brooke, the Home Secretary, went straight home. No one asked him to stay and he knew nothing of the events of the rest of the night. But the Chief Whip had meanwhile seen Mr Profumo. Mr Profumo had been to a dinner and looked into the House on his way home. The Chief Whip told him of the accusations that had been made and said, 'I must ask you point blank, did you or didn't you?' He said, 'I didn't'. The Chief Whip told him that he thought he might have to make a statement, but that he should go back and go to bed. So

Mr Profumo and his wife went home. Their house was besieged by reporters, but they ran the siege and got in about 12.40 a.m., very wrought up, took sleeping pills and went to bed.

The Chief Whip meanwhile had been thinking more about the matter. It occurred to him that these statements in the House afforded an opportunity to bring the rumours to an end and that the right way to deal with them was for Mr Profumo to make a personal statement in the House. He telephoned to the Prime Minister, who agreed. The actual sequence of events is difficult to disentangle but this is what took place. After the debate was over, about 1.30 a.m., the Chief Whip asked Mr Macleod (who, as the Leader of the House, was naturally concerned in any personal statement) to come to his room. Soon afterwards the Attorney-General came in. He took the view very strongly that this was the occasion which Mr Profumo ought to take to deny the rumours. Mr Profumo had been waiting for an opportunity to bring a libel action, but here was an opportunity to scotch them by a personal statement. Next the question arose as to when it should be made. It was agreed between them that it was undesirable to leave the rumours unanswered over the weekend (for the Sunday news-papers would have them without a denial), so it would have to be done in the morning, Friday morning. As they all thought it was desirable to have first-hand information about what had been said, they asked Mr Deedes and the Solicitor-General to return. With the exception of the Home Secretary, all the Ministers who heard the statements made were present – and also the Chief Whip and the Leader of the House (who had special responsibilities if a personal statement was to be made). It was not a pre-arranged meeting of the five Ministers. It just grew.

It was, of course, plain that if Mr Profumo was to make a personal statement next morning he had to be called back. This took a long time because he could not be got to the telephone and the

Chief Whip had to send his assistant with a car for him. Mr and Mrs Profumo were awakened about 2.45 a.m. (despite the sleeping pills). Mrs Profumo described to me what happened: 'We were so groggy. All he [the assistant] said was, "Look, you have got to come back to the House", and I remember Jack, groping his way round, saying "I must have a clean shirt" and trying to push the cuff-links through.' So he dressed and went down to the House.

The Attorney-General thought that Mr Profumo's solicitor should be there too, and the Solicitor-General agreed. The reason was that the personal statement was to be used as the occasion for refuting the rumours, which otherwise would be done in a libel action. It was understood that Mr Profumo had given instructions to issue writs and it was desirable that the personal statement should not contain anything to prejudice the litigation. Furthermore, the thought did occur to the Attorney-General that Mr Profumo might have made some admissions to the solicitor under the cloak of legal professional privilege – and, if so, the presence of his solicitor would be a check to see that the personal statement was in full accord with what he had told his solicitor. A telephone message was therefore sent to Mr Clogg and he arrived some time before Mr Profumo.

When Mr Profumo's solicitor arrived the meeting split up into two parts. The drafting was done by the Attorney-General, the Solicitor-General and Mr Profumo's solicitor in consultation in one room. The others, Mr Macleod, Mr Redmayne and Mr Deedes were in a room next door. Mr Profumo arrived whilst the drafting was going on. He did not wish to take any part in the drafting and talked with the others. Eventually, by about 3.30 a.m. or 4 a.m., a rough draft was prepared by the lawyers in the handwriting of the Solicitor-General. The Solicitor-General read it out to the others paragraph by paragraph. Everybody said 'That's all right', except that Mr Profumo took one point about his associ-

Sir Peter Rawlinson, QC, at the time of his appointment as Attorney-General by Prime Minister Edward Heath, 1970

ation with Christine Keeler. He asked, 'Do I really have to say I was friendly with her?', and the others said: 'Of course you must. In the face of the letter beginning "Darling" you must acknowledge your friendship with her.' The draft was then typed (which took about 20 minutes). Mr Profumo read it through and said he was content. By that time it was about 4.30 a.m. and they all left the House.

It has sometimes been assumed that this meeting of the 'five Ministers' was an investigation by them about the truth of the rumours, and that it was for that reason that Mr Profumo's solicitor was present to protect his interests. I am satisfied it was nothing of the kind. The Ministers all accepted the assurances of Mr Profumo (previously given) that the rumours were untrue and were concerned to see that they were refuted in the most emphatic way possible, namely by his making a personal statement in the House. It was known that he had been waiting for an opportunity of a libel action to refute them – and here an occasion had arisen (owing to the statements in the House) where they could be refuted by a personal statement. The solicitor was called in so as to make sure that this personal statement would not embarrass any action Mr Profumo might bring.

The reason for the long session (from 1.30 a.m. to 4.30 a.m.) was not because the five Ministers were conducting a detailed investigation, but because of the long time it took to get hold of Mr Clogg and Mr Profumo at that hour of night. The actual drafting of the personal statement and the discussion of it took only about one and a half hours.

The reason for it being done at that hour was the desirability in the interest of good government that these very damaging rumours should be scotched at once and not be given further prominence over the weekend. The thought in all their minds was not, 'Is Mr Profumo's story true?' – for they accepted it as true coming from a colleague – but rather: 'He ought to make a personal statement in the House in the morning so as to refute these rumours.'

There is one thing which should be said in mitigation of Mr Profumo's conduct. He did not seek to excuse himself by reason of the very exceptional circumstances of that night. But his wife made this statement to me:

> This is terribly important. I would like to make a statement about this: I just simply know that, if it had not been for the extraordinary concatenation of circumstances of timing that day, and that early morning, Jack would never have made that statement. I was there and I know about the sleeping pills and the tiredness, and the fact that we were really groping round the house, letting in strange people and getting through loads of reporters still on the doorstep. I sat up in the drawing-room with the cat on my lap until he came back at 4.45 a.m. and he said: 'This is the statement.' I am sure that, had we had time, as a husband and wife, instead of … with a time gun …

I do not consider it part of my duty to assess the responsibility of Ministers to the House. That is a Parliamentary matter upon which I would not seek to venture. But I do consider it my duty to set out the knowledge which the Ministers had at the time when they drafted and approved the personal statement made by Mr Profumo, the considerations which were present in their minds, and the steps they took to satisfy themselves of its truth. The two Ministers who had most to do with it were the Chief Whip and the Attorney-General. The Solicitor-General did a fair amount, but as assisting the Attorney-General.

Their evidence before me disclosed these matters:

- They knew the rumours about Mr Profumo, which, stated shortly, were these: (a) the rumour as to immorality: that Mr Profumo had had an illicit association with Christine Keeler; (b) the rumour as to security: that the Russian Ivanov had also had an association with her about the same time; (c) the rumour as to the perversion of justice: that Mr Profumo had helped her to disappear. Only this last rumour – concerning the disappearance – had been raised in the House that night, but they felt that all the rumours should be dealt with in the statement.

- Regarding the rumour as to immorality: They knew the sort of girl that Christine Keeler was now, but Mr Profumo said that, at the time he knew her, she was very different. They knew, on his own admission, that he had been to Stephen Ward's flat on several occasions when Christine Keeler was amongst the guests, and that, on two occasions, they were alone together before the other guests arrived. They knew, on his own admission, that he had written her a letter starting 'Darling', but he said that it was simply a short note saying that he could not come to a cocktail party. They knew she had told her story to a newspaper and had handed the newspaper the 'Darling' letter.

- They had very much in mind the case of Mr Galbraith, who had been assailed by rumours and resigned. The rumours had turned out to be utterly false and they did not want a repetition of anything of the kind.

- They were of opinion that a Minister ought not to stay in office if there are scandalous rumours about him which he is not prepared to answer. The scandal which loomed large in their minds was the illicit association with Christine Keeler. The security aspect of the Russian was quite incidental; so also was the disappearance of Christine Keeler. It was essential, therefore, that Mr Profumo should take the earliest opportunity of answering the scandal of his association with Christine Keeler.

- In answering the scandal they considered this one point to be crucial: Had Mr Profumo in fact committed adultery with Christine Keeler or not? They took it that if he had not in fact committed adultery, the rumour lacked foundation. It would incidentally clear the other rumours, too: for if he had not committed adultery, he was not a security risk and there was no motive for helping her disappear. It may be questioned, however, whether that was the crucial point. The real point may be not whether Mr Profumo had in fact committed adultery, but whether his conduct (proved or admitted) was such as to lead ordinary people reasonably to believe that he had. If that were the real point, the disarming answer of Mr Profumo will be remembered: 'Nobody will believe that I didn't sleep with her, but it happens to be true.' It is for Parliament to consider what was the proper point for consideration, though I may perhaps illustrate the point by an analogy drawn from the civil law. If a man commits adultery, his wife may have just cause for leaving him; but it does not depend on his in fact committing adultery. If he associated with another woman in such circumstances that, on the proved or admitted facts, his wife reasonably believes he has committed adultery, his wife has just cause for leaving him. The reason is because his conduct is such as to destroy the confidence and trust which should subsist between them.

- In considering this one point (whether Mr Profumo had in fact committed adultery) they did not regard themselves as conducting an investigation or inquiry but rather as being concerned to protect a colleague from rumours with which (if his assurances were accepted) he had been improperly assailed. The Law Officers tested his assurances as a lawyer would his client, by telling him to be absolutely frank with them, asking him questions, eliciting answers and considering his conduct. Then, having come to the conclusion that his assurances could and should be accepted, they felt they should go no further. The Chief Whip tested his assurances in a commonsense way and also accepted them. It is a matter for Parliament to consider whether they should have gone further. I only record the fact that they did not have a sight of the 'Darling' letter. They did not ask the newspaper to let them see it, nor did they ask Mr Profumo to get it for them. (The Attorney-General told me he felt it would be improper, on behalf of a prospective plaintiff, to ask a prospective defendant what evidence he had.) I also record the fact that they had no knowledge of the statement made by Christine Keeler to the police on 26th January 1963, nor of the one made by Stephen Ward to the police on 5th February 1963, which was passed to the Security Service on 7th February 1963. (Both the Chief Whip and the Attorney-General told me that if they had had those statements they might have taken a very different view: They might not have been content to take Mr Profumo's word and they might have insisted on going further – for instance, confronting Mr Profumo with them. Mr Profumo told me that if he had been faced with them, he, too, might have taken a different attitude.)

- They were all conscious of the very damaging situation which would arise if Mr Profumo was not telling the truth and that is why they tested it, as far as they felt they possibly could, before accepting it.

The Leader of the House (Mr Iain Macleod) and the Minister without Portfolio (Mr William Deedes) had much less to do with the matter. They had heard the rumours but had taken no part until this night. They had no special knowledge and they participated in the meeting for these reasons: Mr Macleod because he was the Leader of the House and specially concerned if a personal statement was to be made; and Mr Deedes because he was on the Front Bench, had heard all that had been said in the House and was able to give a first-hand account of it. They did not regard this meeting in the least as an investigation or inquiry, but only as a refutation of rumours by a Minister whose reputation had been unjustly assailed.

The Home Secretary left the House immediately after the debate ended and went home. He was not called back to the meet-

ing. The question has been asked why he was not called back. The answer is that no one thought of it. He had never been in the picture previously. It never occurred to the Chief Whip or the Attorney-General that he was concerned in any way. The meeting was concerned with a personal statement regarding a Minister's reputation. It was not regarded as a security matter, except incidentally. Even if it had been regarded as a security matter, they would have thought that it was the responsibility of the Prime Minister and not a matter for the Home Secretary.

This seems to have been a common understanding at that time. The Directive of Sir David Maxwell Fyfe of 24th September 1952 (which makes the Director-General of the Security Service responsible to the Home Secretary but with a right of direct access to the Prime Minister) had never been announced, and it does not seem to have been generally known. Apart from the security aspect there was the disappearance of a witness. That, too, was regarded as only incidental to the essential concern of the meeting, which was to refute the rumours with which a Minister had been assailed. So no one thought of calling back the Home Secretary.

On the morning of Friday, 22nd March, at 9.30 a.m. the Chief Whip and the Attorney-General called on the Prime Minister and discussed with him the draft statement. The Prime Minister approved it after making two minor amendments. As the Chief Whip and his Private Secretary had kept him informed of the rumours and of what Mr Profumo said about them, he had been fully aware of all that had taken place since early February 1963. But the Prime Minister had never at any time discussed these rumours with Mr Profumo. He told me that the reasons were twofold: First, if a Prime Minister sees a Minister and asks a question of this kind, there is no 'follow-up'. The Prime Minister could either believe it or disbelieve it; and if he disbelieved it, he could not do business again as a Prime Minister with him. Secondly, he thought it better to get friends of his own age, the Attorney-General, the Chief Whip and others, to talk to him. If there was anything in it, he would say it to them. Over this period the Prime Minister was told repeatedly that Mr Profumo stuck absolutely by his story. And when he was told that Mr Profumo was prepared to make a personal statement in the House, the Prime Minister was satisfied completely of the truth of it.

The personal statement itself

Shortly after 11 a.m. on Friday, 22nd March 1963 Mr Profumo made his personal statement to the House. The Prime Minister, the Leader of the House and the Attorney-General sat beside him when he rose to make it. It was in these terms:

> With permission, Sir, I wish to make a personal statement. I under-stand that in the debate on the Consolidated Fund Bill last night, under protection of Parliamentary privilege, the Hon. Gentlemen the Members for Dudley (Mr Wigg) and for Coventry, East (Mr Crossman) and the Hon. Lady the Member for Blackburn (Mrs Castle), Opposite, spoke of rumours connecting a Minister with a Miss Keeler and a recent trial at the Central Criminal Court. It was alleged that people in high places might have been responsible for concealing information concerning the disappearance of a witness and the perversion of justice.
>
> I understand that my name has been connected with the rumours about the disappearance of Miss Keeler.
>
> I would like to take this opportunity of making a personal statement about these matters.
>
> I last saw Miss Keeler in December 1961 and I have not seen her since. I have no idea where she is now. Any suggestion that I was in any way connected with or responsible for her absence from the trial at the Old Bailey is wholly and completely untrue.
>
> My wife and I first met Miss Keeler at a house party in July 1961 at Cliveden. Among a number of people there was Dr Stephen Ward, whom we already knew slightly, and a Mr Ivanov, who was an attaché at the Russian Embassy.
>
> The only other occasion that my wife or I met Mr Ivanov was

for a moment at the official reception for Major Gagarin at the Soviet Embassy.

My wife and I had a standing invitation to visit Dr Ward.

Between July and December 1961 I met Miss Keeler on about half a dozen occasions at Dr Ward's flat, when I called to see him and his friends. Miss Keeler and I were on friendly terms. There was no impropriety whatsoever in my acquaintanceship with Miss Keeler.

Mr Speaker, I have made this personal statement because of what was said in the House last evening by the three Hon. Members, and which, of course, was protected by Privilege. I shall not hesitate to issue writs for libel and slander if scandalous allegations are made or repeated outside the House.

I am sure that the Prime Minister and all Ministers were satisfied of the truth of that statement. They could not conceive that any of their colleagues would have the effrontery to make a false statement to the House. The business of the country could not carried on if a member of the Government could not accept the word of another implicitly.

But one or two members of the House did not accept the truth of Mr Profumo's statement. And I must deal at this point with a suggestion that the Prime Minister himself knew that the statement was untrue. It appears that early in March 1963 Mr Profumo said words to this effect to a friend:

I've got involved with a girl. I wrote her a letter. The *Sunday Pictorial* have got it and it can come out any day. I've had to tell Valerie, the PM, my boss.

The friend seems to have interpreted this statement as meaning that Mr Profumo had an illicit association with a girl and had confessed his guilt to his wife and to the Prime Minister. The friend

told a Conservative MP of the conversation and he interpreted it likewise. He was so convinced of its truth that when Mr Profumo made the personal statement on 22nd March 1963 he disbelieved it. He whispered to his neighbour, 'He's a liar'. And in the division on 17th June 1963, when the Prime Minister's conduct was under scrutiny, he abstained from voting.

I am quite satisfied that both Mr Profumo's friend and the Conservative MP misinterpreted what Mr Profumo said. All that Mr Profumo said to his friend was to the effect that he had got into a difficult situation because of his friendship with a girl, and that he had had to tell his wife and the Chief Whip and the Prime Minister's Private Secretary about it. He never confessed to them that he had an illicit association with the girl. Quite the contrary, he assured them that there was no improper association. And he had never spoken to the Prime Minister about it at all. It is, I fear, such misunderstandings as this which have led to most unfounded suggestions. There is no ground whatever for suggesting that the Prime Minister knew Mr Profumo's statement to be untrue. He believed it to be true.

For a short moment it looked as if Mr Profumo's personal statement had been effective. In many quarters (though not in all) his reputation seemed restored. On Friday, 22nd March 1963, after the statement, he and his wife went to the races at Sandown Park and were photographed there by the newspapers. A few days later Christine Keeler endorsed his statement, thus contradicting her earlier stories to the Press. On being discovered in Spain, she said (in the *Daily Express* of 26th March 1963): 'What Mr Profumo says is quite correct. I have not been in his company since 1961.' On getting back to England she gave her story to the *News of the World* (Sunday, 31st March 1963), saying: 'Certainly both he and his wife were friends of mine. But it was a friendship no one can criticize.' She was paid £100 for the story.

John Profumo and his wife at Sandown Park, 22 March 1963

Stephen Ward also seemed to endorse Mr Profumo's statement. On 26th March 1963 he told Mr George Wigg in the House of Commons about (amongst other things) the Cliveden weekend and added that subsequently Mr Profumo visited his flat on at least six occasions. He said that, so far as he knew, nothing improper took place.

But not everyone was content. Some soon returned to the association with Christine Keeler. On Saturday, 23rd March 1963 the *Daily Sketch* came out with a banner headline 'Lucky John Profumo' and said that 'the spectacle of a Minister of the Crown having to get up to explain his acquaintance with a 21-year-old girl is, to say the least, unedifying'. On 30th March 1963 a French newspaper, *Paris Match*, published an article saying that 'Christine disparaît mystérieusement. Profumo a aidé Christine s'enfuir.' Mr Profumo brought an action for libel in the French Courts and *Paris Match* published a retraction.

On 6th April 1963 an Italian magazine, *Il Tempo*, published an article saying that the name of Mr Profumo continued to be associated – notwithstanding his energetic denial in the House of Commons – with that of a good-looking girl, and that, according to public rumour, John Profumo would have encouraged the departure of the girl. The magazine was distributed in this country and on 8th April 1963 Mr Profumo issued a writ against the distributors. On 10th April 1963 the action was settled. Counsel for Mr Profumo stated in open court that the allegations were unjustifiable and without foundation. The defendants paid £50 damages and all the costs; Mr Profumo said he proposed to give the £50 to an Army charity. (On 5th June 1963 Mr Profumo acknowledged that he had had improper relations with Christine Keeler; the distributors claimed damages from Mr Profumo because of his unwarranted claim against them; and he had to pay a large sum in settlement. But he never acknowledged, of course, that he had helped her disappear. That he has always and resolutely denied.)

Others raised the security issue. On Sunday, 24th March 1963 the *Sunday Telegraph* published two articles headed 'Dr Ward's Links with Soviet Official' and 'The Boil is Lanced'. Stephen Ward regarded these as a libel upon him and instructed his solicitor to issue a writ against the newspaper.

On Monday, 25th March 1963 Mr George Wigg, MP, appeared on television and said that security was the main consideration. He was critical of Ivanov. On the next day, 26th March, Stephen Ward sought an interview with Mr Wigg in the House of Commons and defended Ivanov. He gave a long rambling account which Mr Wigg set down in considerable detail in a memorandum. This shows that Stephen Ward said that his friendship with Ivanov had been used in the interests of the country. Turning to Mr Profumo, he described the Cliveden weekend and said that subsequently Mr Profumo visited his flat on at least six occasions, and that 'as far as he knew, nothing improper took place'. He said that the Intelligence Service knew all about the visits. He was certain that never at any time had Mr Profumo put himself at risk in security matters in his contact with Ivanov. He described the recent activities of Christine and Mann, and he concluded by saying that he wished to convince Mr Wigg that on security matters he was in the clear.

During the interview Stephen Ward told Mr Wigg that he had written to Mr Harold Wilson, MP. Mr Wigg told Mr Wilson, who looked up his correspondence, found the letter of 7th November 1962 and, on 27th March 1963, showed it to the Prime Minister. He said that a security issue might be involved and he thought the Prime Minister ought to know about it. Shortly afterwards Mr Wigg sent his memorandum to Mr Wilson, who consulted Sir Frank Soskice, MP. They considered it of such importance that Mr Wilson passed it to the Prime Minister so that any possible security implication could be examined.

The Home Secretary believed Mr Profumo's personal statement.
He had absolutely no reason for disbelieving him. But it left him
feeling very suspicious towards Stephen Ward. Then he heard
rumours that the Security Service had been so worried that they
had sent anonymous letters to Mrs Profumo. The Home
Secretary felt that he ought to know the facts. So on 27th March
1963 he sent for the Head of the Security Service and the
Commissioner of Police and asked to be put into the picture.
There was present too the Permanent Under-Secretary of State of
the Home Office. The meeting was so valuable that it affords a
useful pattern as to the way in which such a problem – of mixed
security and police interest – should be handled.

At this meeting the Head of the Security Service told the Home
Secretary that there was no truth whatever in the rumours that
they had sent anonymous letters to Mrs Profumo. He then gave
the Home Secretary an outline of the steps the Service had taken
and said that when Ivanov had left the country, the security interest
had ceased. Then he added two matters of such importance that I
set out this record of them made by him the very next day:

In addition to this there had been statements by Christine Keeler
and one or two others that Stephen Ward had urged Christine to
ask Mr Profumo for information about American intentions to
provide the West Germans with the Bomb. If these allegations
were true, there might well be a case against Stephen Ward under
the Official Secrets Act … we thought however that the witnesses
in any such prosecution would prove unreliable and we were not

inclined to pursue the matter.

The security interest in the whole case was limited to Ivanov and his contacts, and it was no part of our business to concern ourselves with what Ward was up to in connection with the girls with whom he associated. The Home Secretary agreed with this.

The Home Secretary then asked the Commissioner of Police whether there was a police interest. The Commissioner said that there probably would be grounds for the prosecution of Stephen Ward if the police were able to get the full story, but he very much doubted whether they would succeed in this.

Two things are to be noticed about this meeting:

- It was the first occasion on which any Minister had been told about the request for information about the bomb. The Home Secretary did not know he was the first to be told about it. He did not pass it on to any other Minister. He thought he was simply being brought up to date by the Security Service.
- The Home Secretary agreed that it was no part of the business of the Security Service to concern themselves with what Stephen Ward was up to with the girls.

Further, it should be noticed that this intervention by the Home Secretary had two important consequences. First, the Head of the Security Service immediately gave further consideration to the question of prosecuting Ward under the Official Secrets Act (for endeavouring to get information) and took advice upon it which was against a prosecution. He decided on 4th April 1963 not to take any action on it. Secondly, the Commissioner of Police immediately gave further consideration to the question of prosecuting Ward, and on 1st April 1963 set on foot the investigation which eventually led to his prosecution and conviction.

On 25th March 1963 the Criminal Investigation Department began to receive anonymous communications alleging that Stephen Ward was living on the immoral earnings of the girls, and suggesting that he was being protected by his friends in high places. On 27th March 1963 the Home Secretary asked the Commissioner whether there was a police interest in Ward. On 1st April 1963 the Commissioner decided that Stephen Ward's activities should be investigated. On 4th April the police began to take statements. They took the statements from many of the girls and other persons who might be able to help. In particular they took a statement from Christine Keeler on 4th and 5th April 1963 which she signed. This dealt mainly with Stephen Ward's conduct, but in it she said that she had had intercourse with Mr Profumo. She said he had taken her to his house whilst his wife was away and she described the house so exactly that one would think it was not likely to have been invented. These are her words:

> When I went to Jack Profumo's we went off the Outer Circle to a house on the left-hand side of a small road. I went up some steps into a square hall where there are two large ornamental animals, I think dogs. The dining room was on the right and the stairs are straight ahead on the right. The stairs bend to the left and on the wall is a picture, of all the things that Valerie likes and dislikes including pigeons and jewellery. Facing the top of the stairs is Jack's office, with a drinks cabinet inside. I noticed a strange telephone and he said it was a scrambler. Next door is the Profumo's bedroom with an adjoining bathroom. I think there were a lot of mirrors in the bathroom. There is a table in the centre of the dining room.

She also said:

I last saw Jack (Profumo) in December 1961. Stephen Ward had asked me to get information from Jack about the Americans giving the Germans the Bomb. I did not get this information because it was ridiculous and could have been made in a joke.

(Note: The question may be asked why these statements were not reported to any Minister. I deal with this later.)

The police took several further statements from her, namely on 6th and 26th April, and 6th and 24th May 1963. On 25th April 1963 they took a statement from Marilyn Rice-Davies. They took many others.

These inquiries by the police got to Stephen Ward's notice and he began to be nervous about them. He took exceptional action. On 7th May 1963 he telephoned the Prime Minister's Private Secretary and asked to see him. An appointment was made for that evening and arrangements were made for an officer of the Security Service to be present.

A note was taken of the conversation. It appeared to the Prime Minister's Private Secretary at the time (and the note bears it out) that the main object of Stephen Ward's visit was to get the police inquiries called off and to blackmail the Government by threatening that, unless the inquiries were dropped, he would expose Mr Profumo's illicit association with Christine Keeler. Here are a few extracts from the note:

Stephen Ward said: 'You see the facts as presented probably in Parliament were not strictly speaking just like that. I fear a change may be forced in the situation. ... I made a considerable sacrifice for Mr Profumo. ... I feel I should tell you the truth of what really happened. You probably know as a matter of fact anyway. He wrote Miss Keeler a series of letters. The attachment was a much deeper one than ... I don't know whether you have any feelings about this, whether there is anything you can do. I know myself here that there is a great deal of potentially extremely explosive material in what I've told you.

Stephen Ward next took to writing letters, still in the hope, apparently, of staving off a prosecution. On 19th May 1963 he wrote this letter to the Home Secretary (Stephen Ward sent a summary of this letter to the newspapers but they did not publish it):

It has come to my attention that the Marylebone police are questioning my patients and friends in a line, however tactful, which is extremely damaging to me both professionally and socially. This enquiry has been going on day after day for weeks.

The instruction to do this must have come from the Home Office.

Over the past few weeks I have done what I could to shield Mr Profumo from his indiscretion, about which I complained to the Security Service at the time. When he made a statement in Parliament I backed it up although I knew it to be untrue.

Possibly my efforts to conceal his part and to return to him a letter which Miss Keeler had sold to the *Sunday Pictorial* might make it appear that I had something to conceal myself. I have not.

The allegations which appear to be the cause of investigation, and which I only know through the line of questioning repeated to me, are malicious and entirely false. It is an invention of the Press that Miss Keeler knew a lot of important people.

It was by accident that she met Mr Profumo and through Lord Astor that she met him again. I intend to take the blame no longer.

That I was against this liaison is a matter of record in the War Office.

Sir Godfrey Nicholson who has been a friend for 25 years is in possession of most of the facts since I consulted him at an early stage.

May I ask that the person who has lodged the false information against me should be prosecuted.

Yours sincerely,

Stephen Ward

To which the very proper reply was sent next day:

The Home Secretary has asked me to explain that the police, in making whatever inquiries they think proper, do not act under his direction.

On the 20th May 1963 Stephen Ward wrote a long letter to his Member of Parliament (Sir Wavell Wakefield) in the course of which he said:

Possibly an inquiry may be necessary when a Minister has not told the truth to Parliament.

Sir Wavell Wakefield passed the letter to the Chief Whip.

On 20th May 1963 Stephen Ward wrote also to Mr Harold Wilson, MP, saying:

Obviously my efforts to conceal the fact that Mr Profumo had not told the truth in Parliament have made it look as if I myself had something to hide. It is quite clear now that they must wish the facts to be known, and I shall see that they are.

On 23rd March 1963 Mr Wilson sent a copy of this letter to the Prime Minister.

This spate of letters by Stephen Ward had their effect.

Questions were tabled in Parliament by Mr Ben Parkin and Mr Chuter Ede for the Home Secretary to answer. They were designed to ask him what information he had received from Stephen Ward in connection with inquiries carried out by the Metropolitan Police – no doubt meaning the information in his letter of 19th May 1963 – but these questions were subsequently withdrawn. There was also a burst of speculation in Fleet Street. Everyone there had a strong feeling that the stories circulating about Mr Profumo were true. Things were heading towards a climax.

On 9th April 1963 Mr Wilson sent Mr Wigg's memorandum to the Prime Minister through the Chief Whip. On 17th April 1963 the Prime Minister replied:

My Chief Whip has given to me the letter and enclosure from you dated 9th April dealing with George Wigg's conversation with a Mr Stephen Ward. I will ask the appropriate authorities to have an examination made of the information and will get in touch with you later on if this seems necessary.

(The reference to 'a Mr Stephen Ward' has since been criticized as disingenuous.)

The Prime Minister did have inquiries made of the Security Service. On 25th April they reported their interviews with Stephen Ward and the warning to Mr Profumo. They said:

We have no reason to suppose that Mr Profumo stands in need of further advice about security. ... There is no truth in the story that the Security Service was informed of the dates of, or anything else in connection with, Mr Profumo's alleged visits to Ward or to Miss Keeler.

On 14th May 1963 the Prime Minister replied to Mr Wilson:

Harold Wilson outside the Houses of Parliament, London, in 1963, the year he succeeded Hugh Gaitskell as leader of the Labour Party

I handed all the material to the appropriate authorities who studied it very carefully. There seems to be nothing in the papers you sent which requires me to take action.

Mr Wilson felt it necessary to pursue the matter further. On Monday, 27th May 1963, at Mr Wilson's request, a meeting was held in the Prime Minister's room in the House of Commons. Mr Wilson said he was disturbed to receive the Prime Minister's letter, and that Ward was a self-confessed Soviet intermediary. He said that if the Government were not prepared to initiate any action, he would reserve the right to raise the matter in the House of Commons. The Prime Minister said that all the material had been examined by the security authorities and they were satisfied that there were no unresolved security problems left over. He would however ask the security authorities to look again at all the material and advise him on the position.

The Prime Minister did as he said. He asked the Security Service to look at it again. And on Wednesday, 29th May 1963 the Head of the Security Service reported to the Prime Minister and disclosed to him (what he and his office had not known before) that:

in a statement which Christine Keeler made to the police in January 1963 she said that on one occasion, when she was going to meet Mr Profumo, Ward had asked her to discover from him the date on which certain atomic secrets were to be handed to West Germany by the Americans. It is understood that Miss Keeler denies having ever put such a question to Mr Profumo. ... I am advised that the evidence would not be likely to support a successful prosecution of Ward under the Official Secrets Act. He is not known to us to have been in touch with any Russian since Ivanov's departure. The security risk that Ward now represents seems to me to be slight.

On Wednesday, 29th May 1963 the Prime Minister had a meeting with the Lord Chancellor and the Chief Whip during which the Prime Minister asked the Lord Chancellor to undertake an inquiry himself into the relevant papers. On 30th May 1963 the Prime Minister wrote to Mr Wilson:

> I have been thinking about our talk on Monday. I am sure in my own mind that the security aspect of the Ward case has been fully and efficiently watched, but I think it important that you should be in no doubt about it.
>
> I have therefore asked the Lord Chancellor to look carefully at the security reports and other documents which I have received in connection with this case and to make any inquiry which he deems necessary from the security authorities and the police, and to advise me if, in his opinion, any further action is desirable.

The Lord Chancellor commenced his inquiry on 30th May 1963 and reported on 13th June 1963. Much had happened in between.

Mr Profumo's resignation

The security issue raised by Mr Wilson and the burst of speculation in Fleet Street had their effect.

During the week 27th–30th May the Chief Whip and the Prime Minister's Private Secretary separately saw Mr Profumo. Mr Profumo was told that it looked as if there would be an inquiry. If there was any flaw in his story it would do the Government enormous damage. It was put to him strongly that, if there was anything untrue in his statement to the House, he ought to reveal it of his own accord. He again denied that he had said anything that was untrue. He was told that the Lord Chancellor might want to see him some time the following week.

On Friday, 31st May, Parliament adjourned for the recess. The Prime Minister left for Scotland. Mr and Mrs Profumo left for a short holiday in Venice till Thursday, 6th June. The Press thought something was going to happen. At London airport Mr and Mrs Profumo were inundated with Press men and cameras. They arrived at Venice in the evening. Mr Profumo told me that he had already decided that he could no longer go about with this terrible guilt on his mind. He decided to tell his wife. But they had a quiet dinner together first. After dinner Mr Profumo told his wife the truth – for the first time – that he had had an illicit association with Christine Keeler. He told her all the details. They talked it over most of the night. Mrs Profumo said: 'Oh, darling, we must go home now just as soon as we can and face up to it.' That is what they did. As flying back would attract attention, they left next day by train and boat.

It so happened that at about 9.30 a.m. on the Saturday morning a message came through by telephone to the hotel in Venice saying that he was wanted back a day earlier. That was true. The Lord Chancellor was starting his inquiry and wanted to see Mr Profumo on Wednesday, 5th June. But they had already decided to return.

Mr and Mrs Profumo arrived in England on Whit Sunday, 3rd June, and early next morning motored down to Suffolk to Mr and Mrs Hare (who were great friends of theirs). Mr Profumo told Mr Hare the truth. After taking his advice, Mr Profumo returned to London and on Tuesday, 4th June, he saw the Chief Whip and the Prime Minister's Private Secretary. He said without preamble: 'I have to tell you that I did sleep with Miss Keeler and my statement in that respect was untrue.' It was plain, of course, that he could not remain as a Member of the Administration. He must resign.

These letters then passed:

Dear Prime Minister,
You will recollect that on the 22nd March, following certain allegations made in Parliament, I made a personal statement. At that time rumour had charged me with assisting in the disappearance of a witness and with being involved in some possible breach of security. So serious were these charges that I allowed myself to think that my personal association with that witness, which had also been the subject of rumour, was, by comparison, of minor importance only. In my statement I said that there had been no impropriety in this association. To my very deep regret I have to admit that this was not true, and that I misled you, and my colleagues, and the House. I ask you to understand that I did this to protect, as I thought, my wife and family, who were equally misled, as were my professional advisers. I have come to realize that, by this deception, I have been guilty of a grave misdemeanour and despite the fact that there is no truth whatever in the other charges, I cannot remain a member of your

Administration, nor of the House of Commons.

I cannot tell you of my deep remorse for the embarrassment I have caused to you, to my colleagues in the Government, to my constituents and to the Party which I have served for the past twenty-five years.

Yours sincerely,

Jack Profumo

Dear Profumo,

The contents of your letter of 4th June have been communicated to me, and I have heard them with deep regret. This is a great tragedy for you, your family, and your friends. Nevertheless, I am sure you will understand that, in the circumstances, I have no alternative but to advise The Queen to accept your resignation.

Yours very sincerely,

Harold Macmillan

Mr and Mrs Profumo spent the next few days with friends. No one knew where they were. The reporters searched up and down the country but could not find them. The folk of the village knew. But they did not tell anyone outside. They knew they wished to be left alone.

Mr Profumo did not wait on the Queen to hand over the seals of office. They were sent by messenger. He applied for the Chiltern Hundreds* and ceased to represent his constituency. The House of Commons held him to have been guilty of contempt of the House. His name was removed from the Privy Council. His disgrace was complete.

* A district of Buckinghamshire whose stewardship is a nominal office under the Crown. As an MP cannot resign, application to the Chiltern Hundreds is the conventional manner of leaving the House of Commons.

Mr Profumo resigned during the Whitsun recess. It was announced on Wednesday, 5th June 1963. On 9th June 1963 the *Sunday Mirror* published on its front page a photographic copy of Mr Profumo's letter of 9th August 1961 to Christine Keeler. It had come in useful after all. On the same day the *News of the World* started publishing the Christine Keeler story by instalments. They had agreed to pay her £23,000 for it.

The members of the House of Commons held a debate on Monday, 17th June 1963. On 21st June 1963 you asked me to undertake this inquiry. During the course of this report I have referred to 'Lucky' Gordon and Stephen Ward. It may be useful if I set out the bare details of their trials, but no more, for I do not consider they have any relevance to my inquiry.

At 12.30 a.m. on 18th April 1963 the police received a telephone call to the effect that Christine Keeler had been attacked by Gordon a few minutes before and that police assistance was required. A search was made for Gordon and he was arrested about 24 hours later, on 19th April 1963 at 1.20 a.m. He was committed for trial and remained in custody meanwhile.

On the 5th June 1963 he came up for trial. On the 6th June 1963 he dispensed with the services of his counsel and conducted his own defence. He said he wanted to call 30 witnesses in his defence. The Commissioner, after inquiry, decided that only two of the witnesses could actually speak as to what occurred. The police tried to find these two but could not do so. On the 7th June 1963 Gordon made a statement from the dock. He did not give evidence on oath. The jury found him guilty of occasioning actual bodily harm and he was sentenced to three years' imprisonment.

unday
irror

he Daily Mirror
ewspapers, Ltd., 1963

Telephone :
FLEet-street 0246

Dr STEPHEN WAR
ON VICE CHARGI

ROFUMO'S LETTER TO CHRISTINE ..

ntinued from
Page One

l about his own March 22 Mr. Pro-made a personal nt in the House of ns, saying:
re was no impro-whatever in my tanceship with Miss I shall not hesi-issue writs for libel ander if scandalous ons are made or re-outside the House."

Fair

pril 3 the Editor of nday Pictorial de-hat in all the cir-nces the prudent ir course was to that Mr. Pro-letter would be re-to Mr. Profumo

hat day, in the of Mr. Nevil Henle ard, Chance and Co. ard's solicitors), the was handed to a ntative of Theodore

Goddard and Co. (Mr. Profumo's solicitors) in the presence of an Assistant Editor of the Sunday Pictorial.

Mr. Henle later confirmed that Mr. Profumo's solicitors had thanked him for sending the letter back to its originator.

Four days ago, on June 5, Mr. Profumo made his second personal statement in his letter of resignation to the Prime Minister.

He admitted that he had been guilty of lying, of misleading, of deception, and of a grave mis-demeanour. He confessed that his association with Miss Keeler had been im-proper.

A Photostat copy of the original letter, retained in the Sunday Pictorial's legal files, is reproduced on Page One today.

TO HIS SECRETARY ..

Miss Florence Pearce, who was secretary to Mr. Maurice Grover, a Bristol accountant, for forty-four years, has been left £21,000 in his £205,000 will.

By NORMAN LUCAS

DR. Stephen Ward was charged last night with living on im-moral earnings.

The 50-year-old Har-ley-street osteopath and society portrait artist will appear at Marl-borough-street Court, London, tomorrow.

The charge against him alleges that on dates between January 1, 1961, and this month he lived "knowingly, wholly or in part on the earnings of prostitu-tion."

Slippers

Dr. Ward, as an osteo-path, has treated Sir Winston Churchill. And has drawn many por-traits of members of the Royal Family.

Two Scotland Yard men arrested him at

noon yesterday, walk-ing in Hempstead-road, Watford, Herts.

He was wearing blue slacks, open-neck white shirt, sunglasses—and carpet slippers.

The Yard men, Chief-In-spector Sam Herbert and Detective-Sergeant John Burrows, had called at 6 a.m. yesterday at Dr. Ward's West End home in Bryanston-mews.

But Dr. Ward was not there. He had spent the night with friends at Wat-ford.

It was several hours be-fore the officers discovered this. Then they drove to Watford in a green mini car.

Dr. Ward was taken in the car to Marylebone

police station in London, where he was later charged.

The mini was one of two used by detectives who have been making special inquiries in Lon-don's Mayfair and West End recently.

As Dr. Ward stepped from the car at the police station he spoke to a friend waiting outside.

After the arrest, police

went to Dr. and examine

His arres top - level c Friday nigh representativ Director of cutions.

Dr. Ward, American de pathy, was o become a Parliamentar

BABYCHAM
Champagne Perry

ove a..

BABYCHAM

On 11th June 1963 he gave notice of appeal. On 30th July 1963 the Court of Criminal Appeal allowed the appeal on the ground that there were further statements (they were statements of the two witnesses whom Gordon wished to call) which might have led the jury to have reasonable doubt.

On 1st April 1963 the police started their investigation into Ward's activities. Many statements were taken and a report was made in May to the Director of Public Prosecutions. A conference was held with counsel on 7th June. On that very evening information reached Scotland Yard that Ward was about to leave the country. In consequence Ward was arrested on custody throughout the hearings before the magistrate. These were not concluded until 3rd July 1963. He was then committed for trial but allowed bail, in spite of objections by the police.

The trial of Ward started on 22nd July and continued for eight days. He was allowed bail throughout. On 30th July 1963 the judge started his summing-up, but had not finished it when the court adjourned. On the morning of 31st July Ward was found unconscious, having taken an overdose of drugs. The judge concluded his summing-up in Ward's absence. He was found guilty of living on the earnings of prostitution between 1st June 1961 and 31st August 1962 (Christine Keeler being the woman concerned) and between 1st September 1962 and 31st December 1962 (Marilyn Rice-Davies being the woman concerned). The judge postponed sentence till Ward was fit to appear. But Ward never regained consciousness and died on 3rd August 1963. The story ends, as it began, with him.

Overleaf Stephen Ward arriving at the Old Bailey, 24 July 1963, for the continuation of the vice case

THE OPERATION OF
THE SECURITY SERVICE

The role of the Security Service

No one can understand the role of the Security Service in the Profumo affair unless he realizes the cardinal principle that their operations are to be used for one purpose, and one purpose only, the Defence of the Realm. They are not to be used so as to pry into any man's private conduct, or business affairs or even into his political opinions, except in so far as they are subversive, that is, they would contemplate the overthrow of the Government by unlawful means. This principle was enunciated by Sir Findlater Stewart in his Report of 27th November 1945, paragraph 37, which has formed the guide for the Service ever since. It was restated by Sir David Maxwell Fyfe in a Directive of 24th September 1952 and reaffirmed by every Home Secretary since. Most people in this country would, I am sure, wholeheartedly support this principle, for it would be intolerable to us to have anything in the nature of a Gestapo or Secret Police to snoop into all that we do, let alone into our morals.

Once this principle is appreciated, it will be realized that the only proper role of the Security Service in the Profumo affair was to defend the country against any activities by or on behalf of Russian agents – in particular against the activities of Captain Ivanov. For Captain Ivanov was not only a Russian Naval Attaché. He was also a Russian Intelligence Officer. He must not be allowed to get secret information which the Russians needed. Stephen Ward was a sympathizer with the Russians. He was a close friend among his friends. He should not be allowed to get secret information which he might pass on to Ivanov. Ward was known to be involved in a call-girl racket. He was 'the provider of popsies for rich people'. If these were Ministers of the Crown, that would be a situation which needed watching in case Captain Ivanov might use the girls as a channel of information.

There was yet this further possible role for the Security Service. Was it possible to get Ivanov to defect from the Russians and help us? For, as a Russian Intelligence Officer, he might have information of much value.

When the conduct of the Security Service is examined (as I will examine it in the following pages) it will, I think, be seen that they confined themselves to the role I have described. They had, at one critical point, carefully to consider whether they should inquire into the moral behaviour of Mr Profumo – they suspected that he had had an illicit association with Christine Keeler – but they decided that it was not their concern. It was a new problem for them to have to consider the conduct of a Minister of the Crown, and they decided it by reference to the principles laid down for them, to wit, they must limit their inquiries to what is necessary to the Defence of the Realm and steer clear of all political questions. And this is what they did.

The only criticism that I can see of the decision is that the conduct of Mr Profumo disclosed a character defect which pointed to his being a security risk (e.g., the girl might try to blackmail him or bring pressure on him to disclose secret information). But at the time when the information came to their knowledge, his association with the girl had ceased. Captain Ivanov had gone. And what remained was not sufficient to warrant an infringement of the principle that the Security Service must not pry into private lives. At any rate, it was not such a risk that they should investigate without express instructions.

Ministerial responsibility

There has been considerable misapprehension about the Ministerial responsibility for the Security Service; and this misapprehension seems to me to be the cause of some of the troubles that have arisen. The relevant documents are so little available that it may be helpful if I give considerable extracts.

Up till 1952 the Prime Minister was responsible for security. This followed from Sir Findlater Stewart's Report in 1945. He took as his starting point its purpose.

> Its purpose is Defence of the Realm and nothing else. It follows that the Minister responsible for it as a service should be the Minister of Defence, or, if there is no Minister of Defence, the Prime Minister, as Chairman of the Committee of Imperial Defence. It has been argued that this would place an undue burden upon the Minister of Defence or the Prime Minister, and upon the staff of the Cabinet Secretariat. But from the very nature of the work, need for direction except on the very broadest lines can never arise above the level of Director-General. That appointment is one of great responsibility, calling for unusual experience and a rare combination of qualities; but having got the right man there is no alternative to giving him the widest discretion in the means he uses and the direction in which he applies them – always provided he does not step outside the law.

In 1951, however, a proposal was made to transfer the responsibility for the Security Service from the Prime Minister to the Home Secretary. This was done in a report made by Sir Norman Brook. In March 1951 he recommended that the Security Service should in future be responsible to the Home Secretary. He said:

I believe that Sir Findlater Stewart exaggerated the 'defence' aspects of the Security Service. In practice the Security Service has little to do with those aspects of the 'defence of the realm' with which the Minister of Defence is concerned. And the arrangement by which the Security Service is directly responsible to the Prime Minister is now justified mainly by the fact that it enhances the status of the Service. In practice the functions of the Security Service are much more closely allied to those of the Home Office, which has the ultimate constitutional responsibility for 'defending the realm' against subversive activities and for preserving law and order. I recommend that the Security Service should in future be responsible to the Home Secretary. I believe that it would be helpful to the Director-General of the Security Service to be able to turn to a senior Permanent Secretary for advice and assistance on the policy aspects of his work and on his relations with other Government Departments; and that he would receive from the permanent head of the Home Office support and guidance which the Prime Minister's secretariat is not in a position to give. The Prime Minister's personal contact with the Director-General of the Security Service need not be wholly interrupted as a result of this change in Ministerial responsibility. The Prime Minister would doubtless continue to send for the Head of the Security Service from time to time, to discuss the general state of his work and particular matters which might be of specially close concern to him. And on matters of supreme importance and delicacy, the Head of the Service should always be able, at his initiation, to arrange a personal interview with the Prime Minister.

On 24th September 1952 Sir David Maxwell Fyfe, then Home Secretary, issued this Directive to the Director-General of the

Security Service. This is still the governing instrument today:

1. In your appointment as Director-General of the Security Service you will be responsible to the Home Secretary personally. The Security Service is not, however, a part of the Home Office. On appropriate occasion you will have right of direct access to the Prime Minister.

2. The Security Service is part of the Defence Forces of the country. Its task is the Defence of the Realm as a whole, from external and internal dangers arising from attempts at espionage and sabotage, or from actions of persons and organizations whether directed from within or without the country, which may be judged to be subversive of the State.

3. You will take special care to see that the work of the Security Service is strictly limited to what is necessary for the purposes of this task.

4. It is essential that the Security Service should be kept absolutely free from any political bias or influence and nothing should be done that might lend colour to any suggestion that it is concerned with the interests of any particular section of the community, or with any other matter than the Defence of the Realm as a whole.

5. No enquiry is to be carried out on behalf of any Government Department unless you are satisfied that an important public interest bearing on the Defence of the Realm, as defined in paragraph 2, is at stake.

6. You and your staff will maintain the well-established convention whereby Ministers do not concern themselves with the detailed information which may be obtained by the Security Service in particular cases, but are furnished with such information only as may be necessary for the determination of any issue on which guidance is sought.

After hearing a considerable body of evidence, I found general approval that the Directive of Sir David Maxwell Fyfe embodies the correct principles. I would try to summarize the salient points:

The Head of the Security Service is responsible directly to the Home Secretary for the efficient and proper working of the Service and not in the ordinary way to the Prime Minister.

The Security Service is, however, not a department of the Home Office. It operates independently under its own Director-General, but he can and does seek direction and guidance from the Home Secretary, subject always to the proviso that its activities must be absolutely free from any political bias or influence.

The function of the Security Service is to defend the Realm as a whole from dangers which threaten it as a whole, such as espionage on behalf of a foreign Power, or internal organizations subversive of the State. For this purpose it must collect information about individuals, and give it to those concerned. But it must not, even at the behest of a Minister or a Government Department, take part in investigating the private lives of individuals, except in a matter bearing on the Defence of the Realm as a whole.

The Head of the Security Service may approach the Prime Minister himself on matters of supreme importance and delicacy, but this is not to say that the Prime Minister has any direct responsibility for the Security Service. He has certainly none in day-to-day matters. It would be a mistake for the Prime Minister to take such responsibility because he cannot in practice exercise adequate supervision, and he has not the secretariat for the purpose.

The result of these principles is that, if the Director-General of the Security Service is in doubt as to any aspect of his duties – as, for instance, when he gets information about a Minister or senior public servant indicating that he may be a security risk – he should consult the Home Secretary. The Home Secretary then will have to take the responsibility for further action, that is to say, whether to take steps to eliminate the security risk or to put up with it. If a mistake is made, it is the Home Secretary who will be responsible to Parliament.

It was suggested to me that, when the conduct of a Minister was in question, it would be preferable for the Director-General to approach the Prime Minister direct rather than approach the Home Secretary, because the Home Secretary might find it embarrassing to have to investigate the conduct of another Minister. The majority view was, however, that in all cases there should be a clear and unambiguous channel to the Home Secretary.

Most witnesses thought it was not desirable to set up a Ministry of National Security, and for these reasons: It is important that each Government Department (e.g. the Service Departments) should be regarded as responsible for its own internal security. It would lead to slackness if each Department could feel it could leave its security to others. The Security Service performs a very useful function in advising Government Departments on their security problems but should not take them over. If it be right that each Government Department is responsible for its own internal security, then the Security Service itself deals with national security as a whole. The great body of opinion before me was that this should be dealt with as the responsibility of the Home Secretary and not as the responsibility of a separate Minister.

It was on 20th January 1961 that Stephen Ward first met Captain Ivanov. Their friendship developed rapidly. The Security Service soon got to know of this friendship and desired to know more about it. On 8th June 1961 (four weeks before the Cliveden weekend), an officer of the Security Service went to see Stephen Ward at a restaurant in Marylebone. His report said this:

> Ward, who has an attractive personality and who talks well, was completely open about his association with Ivanov. Despite the fact that some of his political ideas are certainly peculiar and are exploitable by the Russians, I do not think that he is of security interest [that means he was not considered a danger] but he is obviously not a person we can make any use of. [Ward took the Security Officer to his mews house where] he introduced me to a young girl, whose name I did not catch, who was obviously sharing the house with him. [This was probably Christine Keeler.] She was heavily painted and considerably overdressed and I wonder whether this is corroborating evidence that he has been involved in the call-girl racket.

The security officer added in the report:

> As we were saying goodbye, Ward asked whether it was all right for him to continue to see Ivanov. I replied there was no reason why he should not. He then said that if there was any way in which he could help, he would be very ready to do so. I thanked him for his offer and asked him to get in touch with me should Ivanov at any time in the future make any proposition to him.

Four weeks later there was the Cliveden weekend, and it came immediately to the notice of the Security Service. On the Monday following the Cliveden weekend, 10th July 1961, Stephen Ward telephoned the security officer and asked to see him. It must be remembered that the security officer had asked Ward to tell him of any propositions that Ivanov made to him. The security officer saw Ward on Wednesday, 12th July 1961. Stephen Ward then told the security officer that Ivanov had asked him to find out when the Americans were going to arm Western Germany with atomic weapons. It is to be noted that Stephen Ward was quite open about this to the security officer. The security officer told Stephen Ward that he should make no attempt to fulfil Ivanov's request and if by chance he obtained any such information through the indiscretion of any of his influential friends, he should on no account tell Ivanov.

Ward told the officer that Ivanov had spent the last Sunday at Ward's country cottage on Lord Astor's estate. There had been quite a party of celebrities there disporting themselves in the swimming pool, including Mr Profumo, the Secretary of State for War. Ivanov had been much amused by their antics. Christine was there. (Ward explained that Christine was the young girl who lived in his house.) Ivanov was undoubtedly attracted by Christine. After the bathing party, Ivanov had taken her back to his (Ward's) house and they had drunk between them two bottles of whisky. Ward claimed that he and Mr Profumo were quite close friends and that Mr Profumo visited him at his London house. The security officer summed up his opinion of Ward in these words:

> I do not think he is a security risk in the sense that he would inten-tionally be disloyal, but his peculiar political beliefs, coupled with his obvious admiration of Ivanov, might well cause him to be indis-creet unintentionally.

The Security Service followed up this information in two ways. First they wanted to get more information about Ward's establishment and about Christine. So on 31st July 1961 they asked the Special Branch of the Metropolitan Police to make inquiries. On 8th August 1961 Special Branch reported to Security Service that Christine could not be identified and that inquiries revealed nothing to the discredit of Ward. The address was in a respectable neighbourhood where any openly unseemly conduct would soon come to police notice. Secondly, the Security Service thought it would be wise to warn Mr Profumo to be careful what he said to Ward; because Ward was voluble and indiscreet and might easily pass on to Ivanov any information which Mr Profumo might let fall. Further, a thought occurred to the Security Service that, perhaps with Mr Profumo's help, it might be possible to get Ivanov to defect. Mr Profumo might be a 'lead in' to Ivanov. The Director-General carefully considered what to do. He felt that he could hardly approach Mr Profumo direct on the matter. So on 31st July 1961 he spoke to Sir Norman Brook about it. Sir Norman was the Secretary of the Cabinet and was in a position to speak to a Minister on it. He did speak to Mr Profumo (I have dealt with this in an earlier chapter).

It has been widely assumed that the Security Service knew that Christine Keeler was having an affair with Mr Profumo and Captain Ivanov at the same time; that they reported this to Sir Norman Brook; and that their object was that Sir Norman should acquaint Mr Profumo with the danger in the situation. If the Security Service had had such knowledge I should have thought it was one of those matters of extreme delicacy where they might approach the Prime Minister direct; or, if they had reported it to Sir Norman, I would have thought that Sir Norman should have reported it to the Prime Minister. In failing to do so, he would have made a mistake, as Lord Radcliffe said in a television inter-

A queue of people waiting outside Her Majesty's Stationery Office in London for their copy of Lord Denning's report on the day it went on sale, 26 September 1963

view. But I am satisfied that the Security Service did not know that Christine Keeler was having an affair with Mr Profumo or even with Captain Ivanov. They knew she was Stephen Ward's mistress in the house that was all. Their two purposes at this time were (1) to warn Mr Profumo to be careful what he said to Stephen Ward, and (2) to see if there was a 'lead in' to Captain Ivanov. It would hardly seem to need the intervention of the Prime Minister for these purposes.

It has been said that the Security Service ought to have done differently. They ought to have set a watch on Ward's house or got permission to tap his telephone calls, for they would then have discovered that Mr Profumo was having an affair with Christine Keeler at Stephen Ward's house and that Captain Ivanov was often at the house too. But I am satisfied that this criticism is mistaken. The Security Service knew all that they needed to know about the Ivanov–Ward relationship: and it would not have increased their knowledge to set a watch on Ward's house. They knew that Ivanov was a Russian Intelligence Officer. They already had from other sources information as to Ivanov's visits to and relations with Ward. They knew also that Mr Profumo was on occasions visiting Ward's house. They acted on that information by having Mr Profumo warned. I do not think the Security Service should be blamed for not doing more.

From November 1961 to May 1962 many people were beginning to be suspicious of Stephen Ward. At a party at the Soviet Embassy he seemed very much at home. In talking to patients he was obviously sympathetic to the Communist régime. Several thought that he was a security risk. Reports began to come into the Security Service; and also to the Special Branch of the Metropolitan Police, who passed them on to the Security Service. So Ward himself approached the Security Service – no doubt so as to get in first. On 28th May 1962 he saw the same security officer, who reported that:

more than once Ward assured me that if Ivanov ever attempted to make use of him for any illegal purpose, or if he showed any inclination to defect, he would get in touch with me immediately. … my impression of Ward remains the same … he is in my opinion basically a decent fellow despite the fact that he has accepted as true much of the propaganda pumped into him by Ivanov.

I do not believe he is a Communist but there is no doubt that he holds queer opinions about Russia's aims in international affairs. I do not believe that he would wittingly be disloyal to this country but at the same time I recognize that he might well do considerable harm without intending it. One of his very obvious faults is that he talks too much.

The Security Service followed this up by making sure that the Foreign Office knew about Ward. On 12th June 1962 they wrote to the Foreign Office and also saw them; and warned them that Ivanov was a member of the Russian Intelligence Service and that Ward was both naïve and indiscreet.

A few months later reports began to come in to the Security Service, too, about Ward's immoral activities. On 4th October 1962 they were informed: 'From what I hear of Ward and his dealings with women and his enormous circle of friends, I strongly suspect that he is the provider of popsies for rich people.'

Then came the Cuban crisis. The Russians were carrying nuclear arms to Cuba and the United States were about to intercept the ships. The critical days were from Wednesday, 24th October 1962 when the Russian ships were heading for Cuba until Sunday, 28th October 1962 when they turned back. During this time Ward made frantic efforts, at Ivanov's request, to get the United Kingdom to intervene. He wanted Her Majesty's Government to take an independent initiative and summon a summit conference.

By this time the Foreign Office were becoming very suspicious of Ward and asked the Security Service for information about him. On 2nd November 1962 the security officer (the same one who had always seen Ward) told the Foreign Office:

He has a number of titled and influential friends and patients, including several members of the Cabinet. It was this fact which led us to pay some attention to him because we felt he might acquire delicate information from them which would find its way to Ivanov. Ward is a talkative extrovert; he looks upon Ivanov as a real friend; he is also a man of few morals and is said to have provided some of his influential friends with highly satisfactory young mistresses. It is not easy to assess Ward's security reliability but we believe he is probably not a man who would be actively disloyal but that he is so under the influence of Ivanov that it would be most unwise to trust him.

It is quite plain to me that throughout 1962 the Security Service were keeping a close watch on the activities of Ward and Ivanov and were keeping the Foreign Office very properly informed on the matter.

The Security Service in 1963: three important decisions

The Edgecombe shooting incident did not affect the Security Service directly, but, as I have said earlier, it was the cause of Christine Keeler going to the newspapers and selling her story, with the consequence that Ward got very worried. He saw Ivanov on 18th January 1963 and it is reasonable to infer that he warned Ivanov that the story might 'break' soon. Within a day or two Ivanov made arrangements to leave England, far earlier than expected. About 22nd January 1963 the Security Service got to know that he was leaving on 29th January 1963 and he in fact left on that day.

Meanwhile the imminent publicity had got to the ears of Mr Profumo. In the evening of 28th January 1963 at 5.30 p.m. Lord Astor had alerted Mr Profumo to the danger. And immediately Mr Profumo asked the Head of the Security Service to come and see him. He did so at 6.45 p.m. The purpose of Mr Profumo (as at any rate it appeared to the Head of the Security Service) was to see if he could do anything to stop publication of Christine Keeler's story in the newspapers. He gave the Director-General an account of his acquaintanceship with Ward, in the course of which he had met Ivanov and Christine. He described the bathing party at Cliveden. He said that he had visited Ward's flat in Wimpole Mews on a number of occasions, generally when there had been parties there, but once or twice he had found Christine was a drug addict. He said that he had been warned that the papers had got a story in which she alleged an association with him and might also bring in Ivanov's name saying that he was a Russian spy.

Mr Profumo said he remembered that when Sir Norman Brook

had cautioned him about Stephen Ward (on 9th August 1961) Sir Norman had hinted that the Security Service might try to get Ivanov into its employment. (It occurred to the Head of the Security Service that Mr Profumo hoped that the Security Service had Ivanov in their employ; and that they might, in the interest of security, ask the newspapers not to run the story.) The Head of the Security Service told Mr Profumo that they had not enlisted Ivanov for their work, so Mr Profumo did not pursue the point. But the Head of the Security Service formed the impression that Mr Profumo's object in asking to see him was to get a D-notice or something to stop publication, which was a vain hope.

On 28th and 29th January 1963 more reports were coming in to the Security Service (from a secret source considered reliable) about Ward and his activities. They learnt now for the first time that Mr Profumo was said to have an association with Christine Keeler. They were told that Ward had stated that the girl had been visited several times by Mr John Profumo and by the Russian Assistant Naval Attaché, Captain Ivanov; that Mr Profumo subsequently had a prolonged affair with Christine Keeler and two very amorous letters signed by him had been given by her to the *Sunday Pictorial*: that the Russians were so certain that a scandal was brewing that Ivanov had been told to leave on 29th January 1963. (The Security Service already knew that Ivanov was leaving on 29th January 1963.) It should be noticed that Stephen Ward said on several occasions that he told the Security Service of the association as long ago as 12th July 1961, but I am satisfied he did not tell them anything about it and they learnt it now for the first time.

On the morning of 1st February 1963 these reports were considered by the Head of the Security Service with some of his senior officers. He came to this important decision: It was not within the proper scope of the Security Service to inquire into these matters. These were his reasons:

He thought it was possible that Christine Keeler had been Mr Profumo's mistress. But he did not think it was the function of the Security Service to find out whether she was his mistress or not. It was a purely personal side of his life which the Security Service were not concerned to look into.

It would be a security matter if Mr Profumo was sharing a mistress with a Russian Naval Attaché – if it meant that there was a flow of secret information passing through her from one to the other. But Ivanov had now left the country. So any present risk had gone. And there was no reason to suppose that any information had passed from Mr Profumo through the girl. Mr Profumo, whatever might be his private life, was a wholly reliable Secretary of State for War and it was not to be supposed that he had given away secret information. The only security point was the possible leakage of information through Stephen Ward to Ivanov. As to this, Mr Profumo had been warned by Sir Norman Brook and there was no reason to think that he had not heeded the warning.

So on 1st February 1963 the Head of the Security Service gave this important ruling:

> Until further notice no approach should be made to anyone in the Ward *galère*, or to any other outside contact in respect of it. If we are approached, we listen only.

In the evening of 1st February 1963 there was an important call from Admiralty House to the Security Service. The Director-General had already left, so the Deputy Director-General went round. The Prime Minister's Principal Private Secretary told him of a call by a senior newspaper executive who had said that a story had been sold by a girl to a newspaper and it would include passages in which she was involved with Mr Profumo and in which the Russian Assistant Naval Attaché also figured. The Deputy

Director-General said it was recognizably the same story as they already had, and it was agreed that the first step was to see Mr Profumo and see if there was any truth in it. The Private Secretary said he would tell the Chief Whip and the Prime Minister.

It is to be noted that the object of the Prime Minister's Private Secretary was simply to tell the Security Service about the call of the newspaper executive and to get any information which might be useful for him (the Private Secretary) to report to the Prime Minister. His object was not to ask the Security Service for a report, as some might think from what the Prime Minister said in the House of Commons on 17th June 1963. The Security Service did not understand that they were to make a report. Nor indeed that anything more was required of them at that stage.

Meanwhile one of the officers of the Security Service had prepared a minute which came before the Head of the Security Service on 4th February 1963. It is filled, as he told me, with prophetic insight. It is of much importance and I set it out in full:

> If a scandal results from Mr Profumo's association with Christine Keeler, there is likely to be a considerable political rumpus in the present climate produced by the Radcliffe Tribunal. If in any subsequent inquiries we were found to have been in possession of this information about Profumo and to have taken no action on it, we would, I am sure, be subject to much criticism for failing to bring it to light. I suggest that this information be passed to the Prime Minister and you might also like to consider whether or not, before doing so, we should interview Miss Keeler.

The Head of the Security Service considered this minute and discussed it with his Deputy. They appreciated the point that if a scandal resulted from Christine Keeler's association with Mr Profumo there was likely to be a considerable political rumpus –

but they thought that that was essentially a political matter which was now in the hands of the politicians and not the concern of the Security Service. They knew that Admiralty House were in possession of the story and had decided to confront Mr Profumo with it. The Head of the Security Service felt that the action which the officer was suggesting was leading them outside the proper function of the Security Service and that he ought to pull him back a bit. So he issued a firm instruction not to go into it:

> The allegations there referred to are known to Admiralty House.
> No inquiries on this subject should be made by us.

Thus the important decision was made that the Security Service should not pursue any investigation in the matter. In particular they should not interview Christine Keeler.

On 7th February 1963 the Commander of Special Branch went to see the Security Service with the report of the Marylebone officers of 5th February 1963. This report showed that the police had been told by Christine Keeler on 26th January that there was an illicit association between herself and Mr Profumo, that she had met Captain Ivanov on a number of occasions, and that Stephen Ward had asked her to discover from Mr Profumo the date on which atomic secrets were to be handed to Western Germany. Further, that the police had also been told a good deal by Stephen Ward on 5th February. The matter was discussed by the Commander of Special Branch with a senior officer of the Security Service (who had been at the previous discussions and who knew of the decision that had been made). They decided that there was no security interest involved such as to warrant any further steps being taken. The papers were put before the Deputy Director-General, who agreed with the decision and wrote this minute:

No action on this at present. Please keep me informed of any developments.

That decision was of crucial importance: it meant that the important statements of 26th January and 5th February 1963 never got any further. They never got to the Prime Minister or to the Prime Minister's Private Secretary or to any Minister until 29th May 1963. The Home Secretary had some information on 27th March 1963 which I have mentioned above. The question is whether the Security Service erred in not putting them forward. Upon this point I would set out these matters for consideration.

The Security Service were not greatly impressed by Christine's statement about Ward's request for information about atomic bombs. There was no suggestion that Christine Keeler had complied with the request, or that Mr Profumo had ever given her any such information. The only security interest would be a possible charge against Stephen Ward under Section 7 of the Official Secrets Act 1920 for endeavouring to persuade Christine Keeler to commit an offence against the Act. But such a charge would be dependent on Christine Keeler's testimony and it was very doubtful whether this was sufficiently trustworthy to warrant a prosecution.

There was at this point (7th February 1963) no security risk. By this time Captain Ivanov had left the country. They had no reason to doubt the loyalty of Mr Profumo. True it is they might have their doubts as to his moral behaviour – for he might have had an illicit association with Christine Keeler – but that was not a matter for them to report. It might have political implications but it had no longer any security interest. It might have been desirable to warn the Prime Minister about it, had he not known of it. But Admiralty House knew of it. So did the Chief Whip. And Mr Profumo had been seen. They had not been told the result. Nor had they been asked for a report.

Rushing to buy copies of the Denning Report, 26 September 1963

The Security Service had been told in clear terms in the Directive of 26th September 1962 that their task was the Defence of the Realm as a whole, that they were strictly to limit their work to this task, and that no enquiry was to be carried out on behalf of any Government Department unless they were satisfied that an important public interest bearing on the Defence of the Realm as a whole was at stake.

I think that Directive explains the three important decisions of the Security Service at this juncture. The Directive is imperative that they are not to meddle with anything which is not clearly and specifically their business as a security matter and having come to the conclusion, as they did, that there was no security risk involved, they did not think it right to pursue the matter further. I cannot blame them for this decision. The one point of difficulty is whether, having been sent for to Admiralty House on 1st February, they ought not to have followed it up by their going on their own initiative to Admiralty House on 7th February when they received the police report. The Lord Chancellor in his inquiry held that they should have done, and that in failing to do so they had committed an error of judgement. But he did not have the Directive before him, and having regard to the strict terms of the Directive I would not myself find them at fault in not going to Admiralty House.

Nevertheless the fact remains that the police reports of 26th January and 5th February 1963 did not reach any Minister until 29th May 1963, and it has been suggested that they should have done. If the Security Service is not to blame, who is to blame?

I think the explanation is that this was an unprecedented situation for which the machinery of Government did not cater. It was, in the view of the Security Service, not a case of a security risk, but of moral misbehaviour by a Minister. And we do not have machinery to deal with it.

After the three important decisions of 1st, 4th and 7th February 1963 the Security Service took no further part for some time. On 27th March 1963 the Home Secretary asked the Head of the Security Service to come and see him. He wanted to be put into the picture. The Head of the Security Service gave him a full report, and followed it up by considering whether there was any ground for prosecuting Stephen Ward under the Official Secrets Act. When the Security issue was raised by Mr Wilson, the Security Service reported fully to the Prime Minister.

This concludes the operation of the Security Service in this affair. I find that they covered the security interest fully throughout and reported to those concerned. Their principal interest was in Captain Ivanov, the Russian Intelligence Officer, and secondarily in Stephen Ward, as a close friend of his. They took all reasonable steps to see that the interests of the country were defended. In particular they saw that Mr Profumo and another Minister were warned of Ward. They kept the Foreign Office fully informed. There is no reason to believe that there was any security leakage whatever.

Adequacy of cooperation

No one can understand the nature of the cooperation between the Security Service and the police forces unless he realizes that the Security Service in this country is not established by Statute nor is it recognized by Common Law. Even the Official Secrets Acts do not acknowledge its existence. The members of the Service are, in the eye of the law, ordinary citizens with no powers greater than anyone else. They have no special powers of arrest such as the police have. No special powers of search are given to them. They cannot enter premises without the consent of the householder, even though they may suspect a spy is there. If a spy is fleeing the country, they cannot tap him on the shoulder and say he is not to go. They have, in short, no executive powers. They have managed very well without them. We would rather have it so than have anything in the nature of a 'secret police'.

The Security Service in this country is comparatively small in numbers. In some countries there is to be found a massive organization with representatives dispersed throughout the land; in this country it is and remains a relatively small professional organization charged with the task of countering espionage, subversion and sabotage.

Those absences (they are not deficiencies) – the absence of powers and the absence of numbers – are made up for by the close cooperation of the Security Service and the police force – in particular, in London with the 'Special Branch' of the Metropolitan Police and elsewhere with the Chief Constables. If an arrest is to be made, it is done by the police. If a search warrant is sought, it is granted to a constable. The police alone are entrusted with executive power.

I have had evidence which satisfies me that there is excellent cooperation between the Security Service and the police forces. For instance, I have been present at the final stage of a combined operation by which a Soviet intelligence officer was tracked on a journey across the country and his every movement was covered. And I have seen the close collaboration which goes on when a case of espionage is suspected. The Security Service makes all the initial investigations, relying on its technical resources and specialized field force. But as soon as an arrest is possible the police are called into consultation and from this point onwards both forces work as a team. This is absolutely essential at the crucial stage (e.g., when a secret document is handed over by a collaborator to a spy) and an arrest is imminent. Precision of timing is everything. The arrest is made by the police and thereafter the case for the prosecution is in their hands. The two organizations work in the closest cooperation until the trial is over. During the hearing the Security Service tries to remain in the background. This is to keep their officers anonymous and their techniques secret. The recent notorious 'spy cases' show lack of cooperation and should be regarded as an outstanding achievement, rather than as a ground for criticism.

Turning to the present case, it affords a good illustration of how well the forces cooperate.

On 31st July 1961 when the Security Service wished to know something of Stephen Ward's activities, they sought the aid of Special Branch.

In April 1962 when Special Branch received reports that Stephen Ward was sympathetic to Communism, they passed them to the Security Service.

As soon as reports came in of the Edgecombe shooting on 15th December 1962 Special Branch informed the Security Service.

As soon as Detective-Sergeant Burrows of the Metropolitan Police got Christine Keeler's statement on 26th January 1963 Special Branch were informed. There was an unfortunate failure to coordinate within the police force. But on 7th February 1963 (as soon as the 5th February report was received) Special Branch went to the Security Service with the report and they agreed together on what was to be done. The decision may have been right or wrong, but there was no failure in cooperation.

The degree of cooperation which is essential between the two services seems to be a further reason why the Ministerial responsibility should be in one Minister, namely the Home Secretary.

WHERE LIES THE RESPONSIBILITY?

The press, the police and the Security Service

The question now must be asked: Where lies the responsibility for what occurred?

The primary responsibility must, of course, rest with Mr Profumo: first, by associating with Christine Keeler as he did; secondly, and worse, by telling lies about it to colleagues and deceiving them; thirdly, and gravest, by the falsity of his solemn statement to the House of Commons.

But there is a question as to the secondary responsibility. Ought the Security Service to have reported to a Minister the information they had on 7th February 1963? Or ought the police to have reported their information, particularly the statements of Christine Keeler on 26th January and 4th and 5th April 1963? Lastly, ought the *Sunday Pictorial* to have disclosed the 'Darling' letter? Or the story that Christine Keeler had told them? It may very well be that if any such material had been placed before the Prime Minister or the Home Secretary, or indeed any Minister, Mr Profumo would not have succeeded in deceiving them. The Ministers would not have accepted his assurances. He would have resigned earlier and never made his personal statement. Let me take these in reverse order.

THE NEWSPAPERS

It is noteworthy that the senior executive of another newspaper did go to Admiralty House on 1st February 1963 and gave them information on the ground that it was a security matter. It may be asked: Ought not the newspaper itself to have done so, the newspaper which actually held the 'Darling' letter and had Christine's story? They were under no legal duty, of course, but was it not

Christine Keeler leaving court during the trial of Stephen Ward, July 1963

their public duty? If the information had disclosed a present and grave risk, affecting the very security of the country, no one would doubt that it would have been their duty to tell those in authority. So also if it pointed clearly to a Minister being, at the present time, a security risk, it might well have been their duty. But the case does not come as high as that. The 'Darling' letter was, as the newspaper said, 'effusive, but not conclusive'. They were not even sure it was genuine. And they did not know how far Christine Keeler was trustworthy. Stephen Ward had told them that what she was saying about Mr Profumo was quite untrue. In any case it was 18 months ago. It was a story to be told, not a danger to be averted. That is, if the story could properly be published at all. As it was, they decided not to publish it. They changed the policy of the paper and decided not to publish that type of story. I do not think the newspaper was in any way at fault in keeping the story and the letter to themselves, as they did, until after Mr Profumo resigned. After all, many knew the letter existed. No one ever asked to see it.

THE POLICE

It was unfortunate that the police did not take a full statement from Christine Keeler on 1st February 1963 as arranged, or a day or two later. It might have led to further inquiries and brought everything to a head earlier. It might, for instance, have led to an earlier prosecution of Ward and an earlier discovery of the truth about Mr Profumo. This was due to a failure in coordination for which no one individual was to blame. But save for this failure the police fulfilled their responsibilities. The substance of Christine Keeler's story was passed on to the Security Service on 7th February 1963 and thenceforward the responsibility passed to the Security Service. The police did eventually take a statement from Christine Keeler on 4th and 5th April 1963 (while they were inquiring into the case against Ward). This disclosed further details of moral misbehaviour by a Minister, but added nothing on the security issue. And it was not their duty to disclose a moral misbehaviour. The police are not to report upon private lives, even of Ministers. In any case the substance of the story had been passed to the Security Service as long ago as 7th February 1963.

THE SECURITY SERVICE

I have already considered in detail their position. I need only repeat that they work under a strict directive to confine themselves to danger to the Realm as a whole. Once they came to the conclusion that there was no security interest in the matter, but only moral misbehaviour in a Minister, they were under no duty to report it to anyone. They did come to that conclusion. They came to it honestly and reasonably and I do not think they should be found at fault.

WAS NO ONE TO BLAME?

If it be asked why, then, was no one to blame except Mr Profumo, my answer is that none of the Governmental services was to blame. As I have said before, this was an unprecedented situation for which the machinery of Government did not cater. We are, I suggest rightly, so anxious that neither the police nor the Security Service should pry into private lives that there is no machinery for reporting the moral misbehaviour of Ministers. Certainly the police must not go out to seek information about it. Nor must the Security Service. But even if it comes incidentally to their knowledge, as it did here, there is no machinery laid down for reporting it. It is perhaps better thus than that we should have a 'police state'. If that be so, then when a Minister is guilty of moral misbehaviour and it gives rise to scandalous rumour, it is for him and his colleagues to deal with the rumour, as best they can. It is their responsibility and no one else's.

The Ministers

This leaves only the Ministers. What is their responsibility, if any? The case is reduced to this: there were persistent rumours about Mr Profumo, the crux of which was that he had an immoral association with Christine Keeler. The Ministers knew that this was crux of the matter, for it was the point on which they concentrated their attention. If these rumours were affecting the confidence which Parliament reposed in Mr Profumo or the Government, then it was for the Prime Minister and his colleagues to deal with them. The Prime Minister did not himself see Mr Profumo but he left it to the Chief Whip and the Law Officers. These Ministers inquired of Mr Profumo whether there was any impropriety in his association with Christine Keeler. He repeatedly assured them that there was no impropriety, and in the end they were satisfied too. All were clearly acting with the utmost honesty and good faith; their integrity is beyond question.

Nevertheless, there are two matters which Parliament may wish to consider further:

- Did the Ministers ask themselves the proper question? They concentrated their attention on the matter of immorality. And the one question they asked themselves was whether Mr Profumo had in fact committed adultery. Whereas the proper question may have been: was his conduct, proved or admitted, such as to lead ordinary people reasonably to believe that he had committed adultery? If that were the proper question the answer was clear. His conduct was such as to lead to that belief. And no further inquiries would help.
- Ought further inquiries to have been made? The Ministers did not know of the statements made to the police and could hardly be expect-

ed to ask for them. But they did know of the 'Darling' letter. It was possible, I should have thought, for them to ask the newspaper to let them see it, or, better still, to get Mr Profumo to ask them. After all, it was his copyright. Whether the newspaper would have complied, we do not know. They were never asked. If the Ministers had seen it, it might have turned the scale between belief and disbelief of Mr Profumo's word. At any rate, there would have been a considerable risk in accepting his word without knowing what the letter contained.

Those are questions which I would not seek to answer. They are matters for Parliament and not for me. Nevertheless, the fact remains that the conduct of Mr Profumo was such as to create, amongst an influential section of the people, a reasonable belief that he had committed adultery with such a woman in such circumstances as the case discloses. It was the responsibility of the Prime Minister and his colleagues, and of them only, to deal with this situation, and they did not succeed in doing so.

Editor's note: On 23 June 1963 Mr Macmillan wrote to the Queen to express his 'deep regret' over the events:

> I feel that I ought to apologise to You for the undoubted injury done by the terrible behaviour of one of Your Majesty's Secretaries of State upon not only the Government but, perhaps, more serious, one of the great Armed Forces. … I had of course no idea of the strange underworld in which other people, alas, besides Mr Profumo, have allowed themselves to become entrapped. … I begin to suspect in all these wild accusations against many people, Ministers and others, something in the nature of a plot to destroy the established system. …What is so painful to me is to think that, whether by some action or inaction on my part, I may have contributed to the burden. (Letter released at the Public Record Office, March 2003)

Overleaf John Profumo driving his wife to their home shortly after his resignation, June 1963. He spent the rest of his life working with the poor of the East End of London and was awarded the CBE for charitable services.

RUMOURS AFFECTING THE HONOUR AND INTEGRITY OF PUBLIC LIFE

The scope of the Inquiry

The terms of reference also ask me 'to investigate any information or material which may come to [my] attention in this connection [The Profumo affair] and to consider any evidence there may be for believing that national security has been, or may be, endangered'.

In announcing the terms of reference to the House of Commons on 17th June 1963 you said: 'It will be within the knowledge of many Hon. Members that, in connection with the recent episode, rumours are circulating which affect the honour and integrity of public life in this country and, if they were true, might point to a security risk. Such a situation cannot be tolerated.'

I have felt some concern at the scope of this part of my inquiry. There have been many rumours lately concerning the honour and integrity of public life in this country, and I infer from your statement in Parliament that you envisage that some of them might come within the scope of my inquiry.

How far ought I to inquire into rumours? As I interpret my terms of reference I must inquire into them when two conditions are satisfied:

- The rumours must arise out of the circumstances leading to the resignation of the former Secretary of State for War, Mr J.D. Profumo; or, more shortly, they must arise out of 'The Profumo affair'.
- The rumours must be such that, if true, they may give rise to the belief that national security has been or may be endangered; or, more shortly, that they point to a 'security risk'.

However, there is yet another question to solve on the first con-

Christine Keeler, shortly after her release from jail, June 1964. She was sentenced to nine months' imprisonment for obstructing the course of justice in the case of Aloysius 'Lucky' Gordon.

dition: when can a rumour be said to arise out of the Profumo affair? Some of the rumours gave rise to no difficulty, such as a rumour that a Minister was associating with Christine Keeler or one of the Ward girls, or a rumour which was traced to statements made by those girls to the newspapers. Those rumours arose directly out of the Profumo affair and no one has doubted that it is within my terms of reference to inquire into them. But there were other rumours which arose indirectly out of the Profumo affair, in the sense that they would probably never have seen the light of day, or at least never have received credence, were it not for the Profumo affair. The admission of Mr Profumo that he had lied to the House of Commons so shook the confidence of the people of this country that they were ready to believe rumours which previously they would have rejected out of hand. No longer was the denial of a Minister to be accepted. The word of any informer, however bad his character, might be preferred to the word of a Minister. And informers abounded. They saw a chance of making money by telling their stories to the newspapers, as Christine Keeler did. Hence rumours spread.

So I had to ask myself whether I was to inquire into those rumours which arose indirectly out of the Profumo affair. And I decided, after anxious consideration, that I should. If these rumours were affecting the honour and integrity of public life in this country, and were unfounded, I felt it my duty to inquire into them and show them to be so. Whereas if they were well-founded and affected our national security, the truth should not be hidden. Only in this way could the confidence of the public be restored. Some of those who appeared before me objected to my investigating rumours of this kind. They said they were irrelevant. But, rightly or wrongly, I held the contrary. I have investigated them. Even so, there were serious questions to solve on the second condition.

WHAT IS A SECURITY RISK?

All the rumours reported to me were to the effect that a Minister or person prominent in public life had been guilty of immorality or discreditable conduct of some kind or other. But it is not every piece of immorality or discreditable conduct which can be said to be a 'security risk'. In my opinion immorality or discreditable conduct is only a security risk if it is committed in such circumstances that it might expose the person concerned to blackmail or to undue pressures which might lead him to give away secret information. For instance, I would normally regard homosexual behaviour, or perverted practices with a prostitute, as creating a security risk, at any rate if it was of recent date. I would not ordinarily regard adultery as a security risk, at any rate when committed clandestinely with a person who was not likely to resort to blackmail. Much must depend, however, on the circumstances. The Vassall Case showed how photographs may be taken of persons in compromising situations. The existence of such photographs heightens the security risk – so also do compromising letters. They would be a most potent weapon in the hands of a blackmailer, even after several years. To pervert, or to attempt to pervert, the course of justice might well be a security risk. The participants would be under extreme pressure to keep it quiet. In short, every case of immorality or discreditable conduct must depend on its own special circumstances, and not least on the length of time past since it happened and the likelihood of undue pressure being exerted. Hence the need to investigate the particular circumstances of every case reported to me, and this I have done.

WHERE LIES THE BURDEN OF PROOF?

This raised an important issue. There was quite a body of opinion to the effect that, where there is a persistent rumour about a

Minister which, if believed, would mean that he was a security risk, it must, as a matter of political necessity, be disproved or he must be asked to resign. An analogy was drawn with the Civil Service where a man may be removed from secret duties 'because after the fullest investigation, doubts about his reliability remain, even although nothing may have been proved against him on standards which would be accepted in a court of law'.

Whilst I appreciate the political significance of the opinion so expressed, I have felt unable to adopt it for the purposes of my inquiry. It seems to me to be most unfair to the Minister concerned. It means that, once he is the subject of rumour, it puts on him the burden of proving his innocence – a thing difficult enough for any man to do – and entirely contrary to what we believe to be just. It is bad enough to require anyone to meet a charge based on rumour – a charge in which there is no prosecutor, of which there are no particulars, where the witnesses speak often enough from hearsay, and when they cannot be cross-examined. It would be worse still if the individual affected had to disprove a rumour when there is no evidence against him.

In these circumstances I have adopted this test: If there comes to my attention information or material which points to a security risk, I have to consider it to see whether it is of sufficient significance to call for an answer. If it is, I must call upon the person affected to hear what he has to say. Then, having heard him, I must consider whether, in the result, it can properly be said there is evidence for believing that national security has been, or may be, endangered. In short, is there evidence which, sitting as a judge, I would think it fit to leave to a jury?

I have endeavoured to investigate all the rumours reported to me in accordance with those principles. And I have to report that in no case have I found any evidence for believing that national security has been or may be endangered. I would like to have stopped there, but I feel that, if I did, I would lay myself open to the charge of covering up the truth. And there would be a danger that, in the absence of detailed refutation, the rumours would persist. I have therefore set out the course of my investigations. But I have deliberately refrained from setting out suspicions which fall short of evidence, or immorality or discreditable conduct which does not amount to a security risk; otherwise it seems to me that my inquiry would be turned into a witch-hunt, parallel to the McCarthy Committee in the United States, and people would be condemned for past sins which are better forgotten and forgiven. I feel that such an inquiry into private lives would be repugnant to the great majority of our people.

I turn therefore to consider the rumours in detail. In doing so I have refrained from setting down the names of the persons affected by the rumours; this should cause no difficulty. Those who have heard the rumours or repeated them will readily be able to identify the persons from my description, and will, I hope, read the refutation. Those who have not heard the rumours are better off. They need read nothing.

Rumours arising directly out of the Profumo affair

These rumours usually sprang from the fact that Stephen Ward met a large number of persons prominent in public life. He met some at Cliveden, some in the course of his practice as an osteopath (where he had a high reputation for skill) and some in the course of drawing portraits of people. Although he only met them thus casually, he used afterwards in his conversation to let fall their names as if they were close friends. The young girls whom he had about him were flattered to be in the company of one so well connected. And when they afterwards told their stories to the newspapers the names were a good selling point.

There was a heavy crop of rumours immediately preceding my inquiry. On 18th June 1963 a French newspaper published a long article, purporting to be from London headed 'Tous les familiers de la piscine du Docteur Ward ne sont pas encore dans le bain' (All the frequenters of Dr Ward's swimming pool have not yet been ducked in the water). In the article the newspaper set out, with added spice, many of the rumours then current. The newspaper is distributed in Great Britain and its contents became known. Immediately after I began my inquiry I wrote to the Managing Director and asked for the grounds on which the article was based and also to be put in touch with his London correspondent. But I have received no reply. I do not wish to attach any special importance to this mischievous article but it contains such a convenient tabulation of the rumours that I quote extracts from it.

This French newspaper accused the Prime Minister and another Minister (who was named) of a political offence, namely, 'd'étouffer l'affaire Keeler' (i.e., to stifle the Keeler affair). This accusation

was quite unfounded. But that is not the point. When the newspaper got to England some persons reading it (presumably their French was imperfect) said there was an 'appalling allegation' against the named Minister. The hearers interpreted this sexually, as they usually do, and said that the Minister was guilty of indecency with little boys. Hence the rumour. It was a fantastic suggestion, as anyone who knows the Minister will appreciate. And it was of course completely unfounded. It just shows how rumours arise.

This French newspaper said of another Minister: 'Il ne fait en tout cas aucun doute que — était en relations très suivies avec le Dr Ward et sa troupe de girls' (i.e., there is no doubt at all that Mr — had some very close relations with Dr Ward and his pack of girls). This is entirely without foundation. The only connection of this Minister with Stephen Ward was as follows.

In March 1962 the Minister and his wife stayed the weekend at Cliveden with Lord Astor. On this occasion they met Stephen Ward. He came to a luncheon party at the house. He had some conversation with the Minister and his wife on portraits and so forth and left about half an hour after luncheon.

On this weekend, during a walk in the grounds, Lord Astor pointed out to the Minister a cottage, called Ferry Cottage, on the estate which, he suggested, the Minister might care to take on lease from the National Trust. At that time the cottage was derelict, with no lavatory or kitchen. The Minister thought it might be made into a suitable place for himself and his family for holidays, and over the next year he took steps to get a lease of it and do it up. They got builders to do work on it. During that year, 1962, he and his wife and family went to the cottage three or four times to see its progress and they had picnics outside, but they did not stay. On one of the occasions the Minister happened to pass Stephen Ward with three girls and said good-day to them, but had no conversation with them. In February 1963 the Minister and his wife moved in some furniture preparatory to moving in. On 3rd March 1963 they went with the children and had a picnic in the snow outside. They never slept there.

Stephen Ward's cottage was about 400 yards away from Ferry Cottage. In March 1963 the Minister heard reports which made him decide not to go on with the negotiations. He terminated them at the beginning of April 1963.

That is the whole of any conversation or connection whatever which the Minister had with Stephen Ward, and neither the Minister nor his wife has ever been in Ward's cottage at Cliveden nor his house in London.

Out of that wholly innocent incident the rumour about this Minister has arisen. There is not a shred of evidence to support it.

In March 1963 there was a rumour that another Minister had lent Mr Profumo his car knowing it was for the very purpose that Mr Profumo might take Christine Keeler for drives in it. This in turn got elaborated into a rumour that the Minister himself had taken Christine for drives in it in Richmond Park. When printed in the French newspaper the rumour got to the most extravagant lengths: 'La prochaine vedette sera certainement — qui a fourni à Miss Keeler les somptueuses voitures avec lesquelles elle se rendait en compagnie de Profumo à d'honorables parties de campagne.' Selon les personnes bien informées — aurait été l'organisateur des orgies qui se déroulaient dans le pavillon de chasse du Dr Ward. Il n'était pas seulement le spectateur passif des spectacles et des démonstrations de nudisme dans la piscine de Ward dont Profumo était particulièrement friand.' (The next victim would certainly be Mr — who provided Miss Keeler with luxurious motor cars in which she went in company with Profumo to country weekends. According to well-informed persons, Mr — was the organizer of the orgies which took place in Dr Ward's country cottage. He was not only a passive spectator of these sights and of the displays of nudism which took place in Ward's swimming pool, of which Profumo was particularly fond.)

These rumours are entirely without foundations: The true facts on this matter are these: During a weekend in July 1961 (probably 16th July 1961) Mr Profumo borrowed the Minister's black Bentley car which had a mascot on it which identifies it. The reason for borrowing it was because Mrs Profumo had gone to the country in their own car. The Minister was not using his car that weekend as he was going (as he often did) to his constituency by train, and Mr Profumo asked if he could borrow it as he had to be in London. The Minister let him have the keys of the car and thought no more about it. Mr Profumo did not tell the Minister the purpose for which he was going to use it. He did in fact use it to take Christine Keeler for a drive or two in London. He pointed out to her the mascot on it and told her that the car belonged to the Minister. He returned the car on the Sunday night. This was the only occasion on which he took out Christine Keeler in the Minister's car. The Minister had no knowledge that Mr Profumo used his car for this purpose. He had no idea whatever that Mr Profumo borrowed the car so as to take Christine or any other girl out in it.

The whole incident was so unimportant to the Minister that it faded completely from his mind. Nearly two years later, when Christine Keeler gave her story to the newspapers, she actually told them that Mr Profumo had driven her out in a car which had this particular mascot on the bonnet. This showed it was the Minister's car. The newspaper believed her story. When it was put to the Minister (as it was on 2nd April 1963) he said there was no truth in it. This was a most unfortunate mistake on his part. I am satisfied, however, that it was an entirely innocent mistake: he had simply forgotten that he had lent the car. As soon as he was reminded of it (as he was by Mr Profumo on 6th June 1963) he corrected it and acknowledged that he had made a mistake.

I am satisfied that these rumours were entirely without foundation. All that happened was that the Minister quite innocently lent his car to Mr Profumo for one weekend, not knowing the purpose for which it was to be used.

THE CUP OF TEA

In this same French newspaper, the names of two other Ministers were mentioned, as if they were in the Ward orbit. 'Des membres du cabinet comme MM — et — y venaient volontiers prendre une tasse de thé. … Or voici qu'on raconte que les conversations mondaines … avaient leur prolongement dans les appartements de Ward. Mais on y tenait évidemment un tout autre langage et l'on s'y ennuyait beaucoup moins.' (Such Cabinet Ministers as Mr — and Mr — are glad to go there for a cup of tea. … It is said, however, that the social conversations … are carried further in Ward's flat. Obviously a quite different language is spoken there and one which is less boring.) These rumours have never got into circulation in England – they were too obviously preposterous – and I need not dwell upon them.

THE SPANIARD'S PHOTOGRAPH

I turn now to yet another Minister (whose name did not appear in the French newspaper) about whom the following rumours circulated which arose directly out of the Profumo affair.

In June 1963 it was rumoured that the Minister was involved with the Ward girls. I can see how this rumour arose. On Sunday, 19th May 1960 the Minister was a guest of Lord Astor at Cliveden. During that time Stephen Ward came up to the house and gave him and other guests some osteopathic treatment. Stephen Ward asked if he could draw a picture of him. The Minister said he could. On 22nd June 1960 Ward went to his house and drew his picture. That was the whole extent of the Minister's acquaintanceship with Stephen Ward. He never went to Ward's house or met any of the girls. But it appears that Stephen Ward thereafter mentioned his name frequently as if he were a close friend of his. Hence people assumed that the Minister was involved with the girls. I am satisfied that there is no foundation in this rumour whatever.

In connection with this rumour a more detailed rumour arose: about the middle of June 1963 it was rumoured that there was in existence a photograph of the Minister in the company of Christine Keeler which was in the possession of a Spanish refugee who worked part-time as a photographer in the night club 'L'Hirondelle' in Swallow Street.

I was able to prove that this rumour was completely untrue. It is an excellent illustration of how rumours arise and spread. There is a photographer who is a Spanish refugee, and a few years back he did take photographs in a restaurant then called the Lido, but now 'L'Hirondelle', in Swallow Street. In April 1958 the manager thought that one of the customers in his restaurant was this Minister, and asked the photographer to take a photograph of him. The photograph was taken without the customer being aware of it. But the photographer did not think it fair to take a prominent man unawares, so he did not make copies of it although he kept the film. When the rumours became current (that the Minister was involved with the Ward girls) the photographer may have mentioned, and probably did, to two or three people that he had a photograph of the Minister with a girl. This went around, and soon it was assumed that the photograph was of the Minister and Christine Keeler.

The photographer at my request searched through all his films, found the film of this photograph and has produced a print to me. It is plain that the man in it is not this Minister, or indeed any Minister. To anyone who knows the Minister it is obvious that it is not he. The manager and the photographer were completely mistaken in thinking it was.

THE MAN IN THE MASK

Early in June 1963 a rumour spread through Fleet Street and thence through the House of Commons that a certain Minister was the 'man in the mask'. It is clear to me that this rumour was the direct result of statements made by Christine Keeler and by Marilyn Rice-Davies. The statement by Christine Keeler was contained in the story told by her to the Press (from which I have quoted an extract earlier). It was signed by her and Marilyn Rice-Davies on 8th February 1963. This is what she said:

> The more rich and influential people I met the more amazed I was at their private lives. Names who are household words take part in the most obscene things. One night I was invited to a dinner party at the home of a very, very rich man. After I arrived, I discovered it was a rather unusual dinner party. All the guests had taken off their clothes. There were both men and women there and the men included people I would not have suspected of ever doing anything improper. There was one well-known barrister who, I am sure, would be willing to make stirring speeches in court attacking that sort of thing. There were also some well-known actors and a politician whom I recognized. The most intriguing person, however, was a man with a black mask over his face. At first I thought this was just a party gimmick. But the truth was that this man is so well-known and holds such a responsible position that he did not want to be associated with anything improper. The guests were not just ardent nudists. Even I was disgusted.

This was the story as told by Marilyn Rice-Davies to the police and signed by her on 14th June 1963:

> About six people have told me [naming a Minister] indulges in weird sexual practices and has been to [naming the host's] parties where he wore a mask. Stephen has told me this and other girls whose names I cannot remember and it is common talk among Fleet Street reporters.

This story found its way into newspapers in this country and also in countries abroad where it was said that a prominent public figure was the man in the mask.

There is a great deal of evidence which satisfied me that there is a group of people who hold parties in private of a perverted nature. At some of these parties, the man who serves the dinner is nearly naked except for a small square lace apron round his waist such as a waitress might wear. He wears a black mask over his head with slits for eye-holes. He cannot therefore be recognized by any of the guests. Some reports stop there and say that nothing evil takes place. It is done as a comic turn and no more. This may well be so at some of the parties. But at others I am satisfied that it is followed by perverted sex orgies: that the man in the mask is a 'slave' who is whipped; that the guests undress and indulge in sexual intercourse one with the other; and that they indulge in other sexual activities of a vile and revolting nature.

My only concern in my inquiry was to see whether any Minister or other person prominent in public life was present at these parties; for, if he were, he would, I should think, be exposing himself to blackmail. I enquired closely therefore into the matter. In particular I endeavoured to find who was present.

Stephen Ward was undoubtedly present at some of these parties. On one occasion there seems to have been more men than women, and he telephoned the two girls, Christine Keeler and Marilyn Rice-Davies, and asked them to come. They came in towards the end of the party. Stephen Ward told them about the

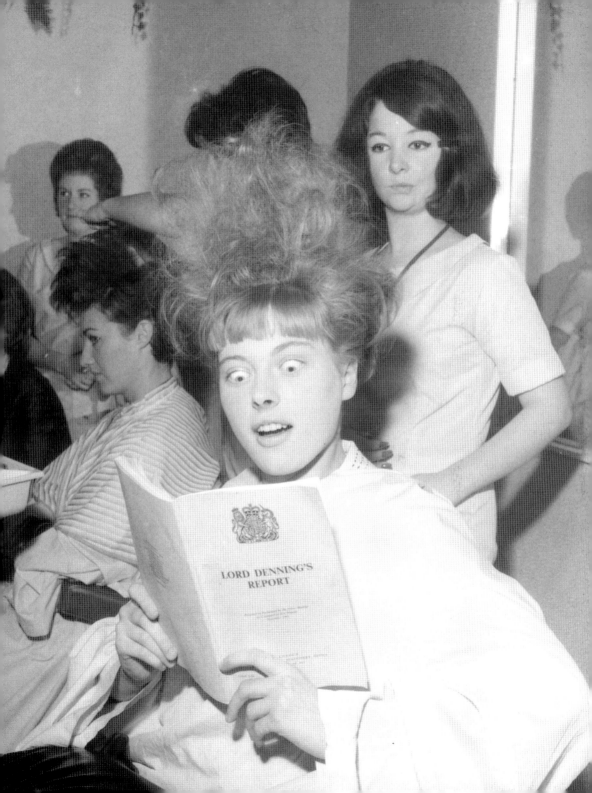

man in the mask and asked one of them 'Guess who it is? It is Mr
—.' Ward seems to have got hold of the mask afterwards and
given it to another girl who tells me she still has it – a black leather
mask with slits which laces up at the back – and he told her that it
was Mr — who wore it. I asked Stephen Ward about this. He
admitted he had been present at the party, but said that no one
prominent had been there. He denied that he said it was the
Minister. He said he had never even seen him. But he admitted
that he might have said in fun, 'I even heard it was Mr — the other
day'. The story soon got elaborated. One of the girls told another
that there was a photograph of this Minister with the mask on and
nothing else, and a little card saying, 'If my services don't please
you, whip me'. Soon it was said that one of the newspapers had
the photograph. All I would say is that I have made the closest
inquiries to see if there is such a photograph, and there is none. At
any rate no one admits having one or having seen one. I have
appealed for any photographs or other material to be produced.
No one has come forward to produce any.

I am satisfied that the events I have described are the origin of
the rumour that this Minister was the man in the mask. It is wholly
hearsay derived from Stephen Ward. He is so untrustworthy an origin – so given to dropping names – that no one should give any
credence to any report emanating from him. But I would not wish
to leave this matter merely by saying that the rumour was not
proved against this Minister. There was much to disprove it. I have
seen quite a number of those who were at these parties. Some of
them were astonishingly frank about the goings-on. One of them
in particular, a solicitor, impressed me with his truthfulness. He
told me the names of many present. They did not include any
Minister or any person prominent in public life. The host and host-
ess and the solicitor identified for me the man in the mask, and this
man actually came and gave evidence before me. He is now griev-

ously ashamed of what he did. He does not bear any resemblance whatever to the Minister who was the victim of rumour.

Apart from hearsay, there was not a shred of evidence adduced before me that the man in the mask was the Minister named, and the rumour was disproved as far as it was humanly possible to disprove it, by producing the people who organized these parties and some of those who attended them. I reject it therefore as utterly unfounded.

I cannot leave this rumour, however, without mentioning that some of the newspapers believed it because of an earlier rumour they had heard about this Minister. It was rumoured that in 1957 he had been involved in an improper incident in Shepherd's Market, about a man who, being chased by a policeman, hurriedly left a house by foot, leaving his car behind. It was rumoured that it was the Minister's car and that he took the precaution of contacting Scotland Yard, announcing his identity, and giving notification that his car had been stolen. I have caused an elaborate search to be made and there is no record of any such incident or any notification to Scotland Yard at all. If there had been any such notification of a stolen car (such as the rumour suggests) a record would have been made of it. There is none. There is therefore not a shred of evidence to support this additional rumour.

INVOLVED WITH THE WARD GIRLS

There have been many rumours reported to me of names of persons prominent in public life who have been said to have been involved with the Ward girls. They were so nebulous that it was difficult to deal with them. Suffice it to say that in every case I found a wholly innocent origin, such as that Stephen Ward had drawn a picture of a prominent person and that he had 'dropped' the name as if a friend of his. In no case has there been a shred of evidence to support the rumour. I reject them all as utterly without foundation.

Rumours arising indirectly out of the Profumo affair

There were in June and July 1963 rumours arising indirectly out of the Profumo affair, in this sense: that they were given credence because of it and became merged in the vast crop of rumours then circulating. For the reasons I have given, I have inquired into them.

THE MAN WITHOUT A HEAD

A certain Minister brought two connected rumours to my attention concerning himself, rumours which I also heard from other sources. They were referred to in foreign newspapers too. He pointed out that these were of a most damaging nature, and asked me to inquire into them:

- That he was the unknown man in an improper photograph which featured in the recent Argyll divorce case, and that a copy of this photograph was in the possession of Stephen Ward. (Another version of this rumour was that the Minister paid a sum of money to the Duke to have the photograph altered so as to have his head removed from it.)
- That he paid money to prevent himself being cited in the Argyll divorce case, and that Stephen Ward acted as an intermediary in this transaction.

As to the first rumour, it has been demonstrated to my entire satisfaction that the 'unknown' man in the photographs was not this Minister. All the photographs in the case have been produced to me. The man's head did not appear in any of them. In order to enable me to dispose of the matter, the Minister offered to undergo a medical examination. He was examined by a medical man whose name was suggested by me and who is of the highest eminence. This medical man proved conclusively that the man in the photograph was not this Minister. He gave me a written report in which he set out convincing detail. He showed that the physical characteristics of the 'unknown' man differed in unmistakable and significant respects from those of the Minister.

Furthermore there were words written in capital letters below some of the photographs; and the photographs themselves, when found, were enclosed in a piece of notepaper on which there were sentences with capital letters. It is clear that the 'unknown man' wrote the words in capital letters on the piece of paper and on the photographs. I have had the handwriting examined by an expert who compared it with a specimen of the handwriting of the Minister, taken without prior warning. The expert was able to prove conclusively that the writing on the photographs and that on the notepaper were by the same hand but that it was not the writing of the Minister. The notepaper was the paper of a London Club, of which it may fairly be presumed that the unknown man is a member. But the Minister is not a member of that Club. There was further evidence before me (which was not before the judge in the Argyll case) which indicated who the 'unknown man' actually was. But I need not go into it here. Suffice it that it was not the Minister.

As to the second rumour, here again it has been demonstrated to my entire satisfaction that the Minister did not pay money to prevent himself being cited in the divorce case. I am quite satisfied that right from the very beginning the Duke of Argyll put before his legal advisers all the evidence he had of adultery by his wife with anyone; and that he told them that they were not on any account to be influenced by the identity of any individual; and that, if there was any evidence against a prominent man, they were not to consider his position. His legal advisers included some of the most respected and honoured names in the profession, and it was on their advice that the case was confined to the three named men and the 'unknown man' in the photograph with whom I have already dealt above. At my request they gave me the fullest information about the case, and I am satisfied that their advice was sound. It was a hard-fought case and no feelings were spared. I am satisfied that the Minister would have been cited if there had been evidence to justify it, and that the only reason he was not cited was because there was no such evidence.

That being so, there was no reason for the Minister to offer a sum of money, and I am satisfied that he did not do so. The Minister freely produced for my inspection his bank accounts for the relevant period, and there is not a trace of any sum of money having been paid directly or indirectly to or for the benefit of the Duke.

I have therefore come to the conclusion that this rumour also is entirely without foundation.

THE INFORMERS

I have yet to deal with two other rumours. They had all these characteristics in common: each of them came from an informer who was of bad character with a criminal record; each of them recounted a story of immoral behaviour in which he or she was a participant; and each of them sought to implicate a Minister in this behaviour. In each case the story, if it were true, could point to a security risk. I have reason to think that in each case the informer had it in mind that, if he or she could convince me of the truth of the story, it would be all the more marketable to sell to the newspapers. Indeed, I was quite satisfied that such was the intention of one of them, for it was proved beyond question. She had, even during my inquiry, gone so far as to enter into a conditional contract with a newspaper and got a payment on account. It was obvious that the evidence of these informers must be viewed with the greatest caution, but, even so, I did not think it would be right to reject it out of hand. The story might turn out to be true, just as Christine Keeler's story to the newspapers was true that she had an illicit association with Mr Profumo. People who seek to make money out of their own immorality may still be telling the truth. So I felt I had to inquire in each case into the story, to test it all I could, to see if there was any corroboration of it, and to put it to the person affected. This I have done. I was satisfied that much of what I was told was untrue. If in what remained there were any evidence of a security risk, I would of course report it. But after the fullest investigation I am satisfied that in each case there is no evidence that national security has been or may be affected.

There I must leave it, without setting out the details, for I am quite satisfied that if I were to do so I would be playing into the hands of these informers. They would, I am sure, go back to the newspapers and sell their stories for a high price. And my inquiry would be turned by them, not only into a witch-hunt, but also into an instrument for their sordid gain. This would be so distasteful a result that I beg to be excused from lending any aid to it.

OTHER RUMOURS

There were other rumours arising indirectly out of the Profumo affair in that they only become current because of it (such as that a prominent person was visiting a girl every week at such-and-such a place or someone else had an affair with his secretary). These again were so nebulous that I found it difficult to deal with them. Nevertheless I investigated them and have to report there is not a shred of evidence in support of them. I reject them as utterly unfounded.

Conclusion

I know that Ministers and others have felt so aggrieved by the rumours about them that they have contemplated bringing actions for libel or slander in respect of them. I know, too, that they have refrained from doing so pending my inquiry. I hope, however, that they will not feel that honour requires them to pursue these matters further. My findings will, I trust, be accepted by them as a full and sufficient vindication of their good names. It is, I believe, better for the country that these rumours should be buried and that this unfortunate episode should be closed.

Equally I trust that all others will now cease to repeat these rumours which have been proved so unfounded and untrue; and that newspapers and others will not seek to put names to those whom I have deliberately left anonymous. For I fear that, if names are given, human nature being what it is, people will say 'there's no smoke without fire' – a proposition which in this instance is demonstrably untrue.

This brings me to the end. It might be thought – indeed it has been thought – by some that these rumours are a symptom of a decline in the integrity of public life in this country. I do not believe this to be true. There has been no lowering of standards. But there is this difference today. Public men are more vulnerable than they were; and it behoves them, even more than ever, to give no cause for scandal. For if they do, they have to reckon with a growing hazard which has been disclosed in the evidence I have heard. Scandalous information about well-known people has become a marketable commodity. True or false, actual or invented, it can be sold. The greater the scandal the higher the price it commands. If supported by photographs or letters, real or imaginary, all the better. Often enough the sellers profess to have been themselves participants in the discreditable conduct which they seek to exploit. Intermediaries move in, ready to assist the same and ensure the highest prices. The story improves with the telling. It is offered to those newspapers – there are only a few of them – who deal in this commodity. They vie with one another to buy it. Each is afraid the other will get it first. So they buy it on chance that it will turn out profitable. Sometimes it is no use to them. It is palpably false. At other times it is credible. But even so, they dare not publish the whole of the information. The law of libel and the rules of contempt of court exert an effective restraint. They publish what they can, but there remains a substantial part which is not fit for publication. This unpublished part goes around by word of mouth. It does not stop in Fleet Street. It goes to Westminster. It crosses the Channel, even the Atlantic, and back again, swelling all the time. Yet without the original purchase, it might never have got started on its way.

When such deplorable consequences are seen to ensue, the one thing that is clear is that something should be done to stop the trafficking in scandal for reward. The machinery is ready to hand. There is a new Press Council already in being.

Although I have felt it necessary to draw attention to this matter, I would like to say that I have had the greatest cooperation and assistance from the newspapers and all concerned with them; and not least from those whose practices I hold to be open to criticism.

DENNING

16th September 1963

Moments of History

2002
The Irish Book of Death and Flying Ships
Marilyn Monroe: the FBI files

2003
The British War in Afghanistan
Escaping from Germany: the British Government files
The Great British Train Robbery, 1963
The Highland Division by Eric Linklater
John Lennon: the FBI files
The Mediterranean Fleet: Greece to Tripoli
The Scandal of Christine Keeler and John Profumo: Lord Denning's Report, 1963
The Shooting of John F. Kennedy, 1963: The Warren Commission

2004
Florence Nightingale
Nixon and Watergate
Peace in Tibet: the Younghusband expedition, 1904
Sacco and Vanzetti: the FBI files
The Theft of the Irish Crown Jewels, 1907
Victory in Europe, 1945: General Eisenhower's Report
War in Italy, 1944: the battles for Monte Cassino
Worldwide Battles of the Great War, 1915–1918

Uncovered Editions

Crime
Rillington Place, 1949
The Strange Story of Adolf Beck
The Trials of Oscar Wilde, 1895

From top right: Illustrations from *John Lennon: the FBI files; Marilyn Monroe: the FBI files; The British War in Afghanistan: the dreadful retreat from Kabul in 1842; The Irish Book of Death and Flying Ships: from the Chronicles of Ancient Ireland*

Ireland

Bloody Sunday: Lord Widgery's Report, 1972

The Irish Uprising, 1914–21

Transport

The Loss of the Titanic, 1912

R.101: the Airship Disaster, 1930

Tragic Journeys (Titanic, R.101, Munich Air Crash)

Travel and British Empire

The Amritsar Massacre: General Dyer in the Punjab, 1919

The Boer War: Ladysmith and Mafeking, 1900

The British Invasion of Tibet: Colonel Younghusband, 1904

Florence Nightingale and the Crimea, 1854–55

King Guezo of Dahomey, 1850–52

Mr Hosie's Journey to Tibet, 1904

The Siege Collection (Kars, Boer War, Peking)

The Siege of Kars, 1855

The Siege of the Peking Embassy, 1900

Travels in Mongolia, 1902

Wilfred Blunt's Egyptian Garden: Fox-hunting in Cairo

Tudor History

Letters of Henry VIII, 1526–29

UK Politics since 1945

John Profumo and Christine Keeler, 1963

UFOs in the House of Lords, 1979

War in the Falklands, 1982

United States of America

The Assassination of John F. Kennedy, 1963

The Cuban Missile Crisis, 1962

The St Valentine's Day Massacre, 1929

UFOs in America, 1947

The Watergate Affair, 1972

The War Facsimiles

(Illustrated books published by the British government during the war years)

The Battle of Britain, August–October 1940

The Battle of Egypt, 1942

Bomber Command, September 1939–July 1941

East of Malta, West of Suez, September 1939 to March 1941

Fleet Air Arm, 1943

Land at War, 1939–1944

Ocean Front: the story of the war in the Pacific, 1941–1944

Roof over Britain, 1939–1942

World War I

British Battles of World War I, 1914–15

Defeat at Gallipoli: the Dardanelles Commission Part II, 1915–16

Lord Kitchener and Winston Churchill: the Dardanelles Commission Part I,
  1914–15

The Russian Revolution, 1917

War 1914: Punishing the Serbs

The World War I Collection (Dardanelles Commission, British Battles of World
  War I)

World War II

Attack on Pearl Harbor, 1941

D Day to VE Day: General Eisenhower's Report, 1944–45

Escape from Germany, 1939–45

The Judgment of Nuremberg, 1946

Tragedy at Bethnal Green

War 1939: Dealing with Adolf Hitler

The World War II Collection (War 1939, D Day to VE Day, Judgment of
  Nuremberg)

(see also *The War Facsimiles*)

UK Distribution and Orders

Littlehampton Book Services, Faraday Close, Durrington, West Sussex BN13 3RB
Telephone: 01903 828800 Fax: 01903 828801
E-mail: orders@lbsltd.co.uk

Sales Representation

Compass Independent Book Sales, Barley Mow Centre, 10 Barley Mow Passage,
Chiswick, London W4 4PH
Telephone: 0208 994 6477 Fax: 0208 400 6132

US Sales and Distribution

Midpoint Trade Books, 27 West 20th Street, Suite 1102, New York, NY 10011
Telephone: (1) 212 727 0190 Fax: (1) 212 727 0195

Midpoint Trade Books, 1263 Southwest Blvd, Kansas City, KS 66103
Telephone: (1) 913 831 2233 Fax: (1) 913 362 7401

Other Representation
Australia

Nick Walker, Australian Book Marketing/Australian Scholarly Publishing Pty Ltd
PO Box 299, Kew, Victoria 3101; Suite 102, 282 Collins Street, Melbourne 3000
Telephone: 03 9654 0250 Fax: 03 9663 0161
E-mail: aspec@ozemail.com.au

Scandinavia

Hanne Rotovnik, Publishers' Representative, PO Box 5, Strandvejen 785B,
DK-2930 Klampenborg
E-mail: Hanne@rotovnik.dk

South Africa

Colin McGee, Stephan Phillips (Pty) Ltd. PO Box 434, Umdloti Beach 4350
Telephone: +27 (0) 31 568 2902 Fax: +27 (0) 31 568 2922
E-mail: colinmcgee@mweb.co.za

Titles can also be ordered from www.timcoatesbooks.com